Word into Heart

Guided Meditations from Scripture
for Personal Use, Group Work
or School Groups.

Anne Alcock

VERITAS

First published 2000 by
Veritas Publications
7/8 Lower Abbey Street
Dublin 1

ISBN 1 85390 479 1

British Library Cataloguing
in Publication Data.
A catalogue record for
this book is available
from the British Library.

Designed by Colette Dower
Printed in the Republic of Ireland by Betaprint Ltd, Dublin

To retreatant, Sr Canice,
who made me promise
I would write this book
before she died!

Contents

Preface

My own introduction to meditation came through word of mouth when I was twenty. At the time I thought that taking up 'meditation' meant abandoning all other ways of prayer, including Scripture. That was years ago. Since then, I have reclaimed Scripture, and learned to distinguish between different forms of prayer, and different approaches to meditation. I use whichever form feels 'right' over a longer or shorter period.

Sitting with Scripture as meditation, and letting its meaning trickle from head to heart, takes practice. But, as someone once said, *How can you practise, or teach others to practise, unless you know where to begin?* The style of meditative prayer presented here involves deep relaxation, a short Scripture text, guided visualisation and prayerful silence. It is a framework that evolved out of thirty-day retreats, and working holistically. I have met many people who, in keeping with present body-consciousness, feel inclined towards body-work and deep relaxation as an aspect of their spirituality. But they still want to keep in touch with, and pray with, Scripture. I have also found that the shift from head-work to body-work, through relaxation, helps young people in particular to enter a more interior space, and deepens their relationship with the depths of Scripture. This book came into being after talking with a group of Higher Diploma students, or teachers-in-training. They wanted to pray with students, but felt diffident about actually getting started. They asked: *How do I get them quiet?* and *I'm not sure I really know how to do this myself – I never relax!* and finally, *Is there a book?*

The New Testament texts are taken from the *New Revised Standard Version* (NRSV). These are 'story-based' and were chosen because their content easily taps into personal experience. This is especially true where Scripture is being engaged with for the first time. I believe that opening oneself to any text of Scripture is always an experience of promise and possibility, and age is no barrier. We recognise at the level of our vision. So whether we are beginners, or those regularly revisiting a favourite text, who knows what new insight will intimate that next step on our personal journey!

Sensing the Real

'Stay where you find the Lord.'

Apart from 'I love you', the most exciting words I ever heard in my life are, *There will come a wonderful moment, perhaps a wonderful day, when Scripture will become so real for you, it will never be the same again!* When I heard this, I realised that hearts actually do leap. I believed that it could be true. I still do. So when people tell me that their prayer has changed, that they don't pray with heart any more, that they feel out of touch, I hear that word 'real' again. If it doesn't actually feel real, who is going to bother to pray? And our experience of what is real has changed. We have become much more aware of our bodies and we are also much more psychologically aware, so there is a broadening of our inner experience of reality. We are whole. The content of personal spirituality concerns the heart and body as much as the soul. The questions I ask myself now admit the reality of feelings. Becoming aware of what these really are helps me to discern where I am going, why, and with what attitude and energy. It brings me to reflect on and collaborate with what we used to call 'God's will', but what Fr Peter Hannon SJ delightfully terms *'God's dream in us'*.

We need to discern and pray as we are, not as we aren't. So how *am* I – in body, mind and spirit? It may be necessary to transcend feelings on occasion, but first they have to be acknowledged.

Being real in prayer tugs off the sometimes masking cloak of language. In the story of the Bartimaeus, we see him throwing off his cloak, coming to Jesus, and hearing the heart-searching question, 'What do you want?' This question can also be put to us, if we allow ourselves to put aside our false self-protectiveness, honestly evaluate our feelings, and meet our own truth.

WHEN, WHERE, HOW?...

Praying imaginatively with Scripture is not new. Ignatius of Loyola used the approach in the sixteenth century, for his 'composition of place' in the Spiritual Exercises. He outlined the image, suggested a visualisation, and gave points for reflection. The rest he left to God and the retreatant. Despite a detailed manual of instruction, his was a wonderfully light approach, trusting the process that leads a person from experience to insight. This process can of course exist outside a formal setting. People often say to me at the end of a retreat, 'It's been so good. I'm just afraid it won't last.' And I always say, 'Everything that happened, happened between you and the Lord. You were the ones who did it. This doesn't have to change.' It is important to realise this. Of course ambience and circumstances will be different, but the heart can remain connected. This is what is called having a contemplative attitude.

This can be true anywhere but, as Fr John Dalrymple once said, 'You cannot pray all of the time everywhere, unless you pray some of the time somewhere'.

You may have the use of a prayer-room, or chapel, or a chosen personal space for your own quiet time. A friend of mine uses her kitchen breakfast-bar before anyone else gets up. It could equally be a window-seat, or a favourite chair. Two other friends pray in a local church, which brings us to the question of when to pray. They meditate during a lunch-break, because that is their only free time. However, dawn and dusk are the times when it is thought that we are most in balance and harmony with the universe, and many people are able to pray then. Are you an owl or a lark? It is good if you can go with your own inner rhythm here. (I myself am at my most attentive at about 5.00 a.m.)

But where does relaxation come in? I don't know about you, but sometimes I am definitely too busy. This busy me is the same me who comes to meditate. Who else? So there I am, over-alert, aware of things that need to be done, distracted by the immediate past, and over-stretching into the future. If this also sounds like you, how do we become present to the present?

BEING THERE

Choose a text that seems to fit how you are. Ask yourself, 'How am I in my body? Where am I in my thoughts? How am I in my feelings?' Not judging, not changing, just aware. Just honest. There is no point in pretending to be how you aren't, and every advantage in coming as you are. Find yourself and you find God is within.

So, read the text through, letting the reading begin to slow you down. Sometimes, as pure gift, reflective reading brings you almost at once into stillness and recollection. If that happens, you probably already know to ignore the relaxation and visualisation. You don't need them. You are already there. However, if you are still in the slowing-down stage, just stay gently with the text and allow it to bring you its flavour and imagery, which you carry through the relaxation into the visualisation-meditation. Here, drawing on your own present experience, the process is a personal relationship with the Lord – a mystery. Someone once said that we only know of God what we knew up to the last minute, and so if we trustingly open ourselves to this un-knowing, the possibilities are infinite. Thus, any seeming 'guidance' in the visualisations that follow is simply a brushstroke to outline, not confine, a theme. At some point the book's words will become irrelevant. Follow your own inner trail through the text and wherever it leads you. The following poem describes one individual's experience:

> Listening to the rhythm within,
> Listening deeply, because it changed...
> The usual, normal, healthy one is there on top.
> Efficient, dealing deftly with daily life.
> But deeper still, is a slower

barely moving beat...
hardly a rhythm.
It is slow; almost still
as if the world were holding its breath
before the next gentle murmur
breaks through the still anaesthetised beat.
Or is it a subtle change in time
alerting me. Alerting me
to go back, and back
profoundly, boundlessly
to be in touch with
The Rhythm before
I was born and loved
in Time?

(Catherine, 53)

I'VE BEEN ASKED TO START A PRAYER-GROUP...
Suppose you want to use this book, not just for yourself but for others, and are asking 'How?'

The good news is: You're not the one ultimately in charge. Once, in Zambia, a group of partially sighted and blind Christians, who were praying with Scripture, asked me, *Are you ringing a bell for us to follow? Do you already know the way?*

They were probably asking this because I was the one who set up the venue and who passed around the braille Bible, but I knew from hearing the truthfulness of their response to the Lord that I certainly wasn't leading anyone anywhere. It was the other way round. Theirs was such a fresh faith. I could truthfully answer, *No, I am learning from your experience.*

So there is no burden of charge; a leader simply sets the scene, reads the text, then steps back.

SCENE-SETTING
In terms of time, you are probably talking about a little over an hour with adults, forty-five minutes with young people. Although

the floor is ideal for the relaxation, for older adults it may be an unnecessary physical penance, so chairs should be as available an option as the floor. If you choose to use the floor, then a sleeping bag, or a light rug folded into floor-padding and top-cover, is useful.

Come early and check the heating. Nothing is more off-putting than trying to pray in a draught, while the heating is noisily but reluctantly stirring into life, and everyone is silently shivering. Soft lighting is good, and if there are only neon strips, then leave out electricity and use candles. Background 'seamless' music or natural sounds are an option.

Explain the timeframe and the steps. Acknowledge that sometimes people fall asleep and that this is no problem. This will ease embarrassment when it happens.

Allow time for people to settle, and then centre yourself. Ask God to be with the group. Breathe, centre your energy. Read the text, very slowly, pausing at every full stop for at least as much as five seconds. Each participant will take what is real for themselves. Then read the relaxation steps even more slowly, as far as possible allowing your body to go with the suggestion too. This calms and slows your voice. As you move to the meditation, let the pauses become longer – perhaps a full two minutes where the dots indicate visualising, and at least a minute at the lesser pauses. Pace yourself, and *allow at least ten to twelve minutes for total silence at the end*, before the guidance for coming out of the meditation.

Remind participants that they can tune you out as soon as they feel themselves being drawn along a path of their own. Remember, each named theme is only a starting point.

You Teach Religion

You teach religion. You have twenty-seven young people who have heard about meditation and are curious. They are begging you to 'please, please, please, show us how to meditate'.

What now?

You want to respond to their and your wish to meditate. But how, and most importantly, where? Without a purpose-built room, this is up to each teacher's ingenuity.

SPACE

The ideal space is 'big enough and small enough'. Large enough to prevent squashing and all that that entails, but small enough to feel inclusive. Ingenuity here might simply mean creating a small prayer-nook in the corner of a too-large room, or removing all furniture from a too-small room. This may also mean arranging to split and share the group with other colleagues, if this is in any way feasible.

Sometimes 'discovered' spaces are, or were, storerooms. They obviously can't stay that way, so the next step is the clearout. This can usefully involve the pupils, as a stage in the whole prayer-preparation process.

FLOOR

Children and young people usually like the novelty of the floor, as well as finding it helpful for deep relaxation. So it should be clean and friendly. Also carpeted. Even with the best will in the world, it is (literally) pretty hard to lie on a jacket on lino or on a wooden floor for half an hour. Carpet cutoffs are kinder. Or a mat.

Whether or not you use the floor or chairs or cushions depends on the size of your group, and your sense of your ability to contain it in calm control. If you have to even think about that second point, use chairs.

AMBIENCE

Ambience is next. Candles? Relaxation-meditation is an eyes-closed experience, but this may be hard for young people, especially in a group. Soft candlelight helps ambience as well as providing a focal point when eyes open. Essential-oil fragrance is fine, provided it is subtle. If not, everyone coughs. If not diluted in a candle-burner, one or two drops of lavender or sandalwood dabbed onto a hot radiator or dripped into the wax of a lighted night-light is sufficient.

SETTING UP AND CLEARING UP

Everything cleared aside needs to be put back. This is so obvious it may seem unnecessary to mention it, but since strategy is needed to get it done with minimum disruption, holding onto calm, and within a time pressure, here are a few tips for anyone starting off.

If a furniture-shift is necessary before the next group of pupils needs the room, a rota-system of three efficient pupils speeds things up if they can get to the room first and fast. If not, in the lesson before the meditation, plan who is going to move what as soon as they all enter the room. Assuming a forty-minute class, the meditation would last about twenty minutes, with the text-reading and relaxation taking about eight minutes. At the end, count on eight minutes to get the room back to a classroom again, and if it happens more quickly, and there is nothing 'to do', keep in the mood by asking the pupils to write their personal evaluation of the experience. I always do this, anyway. This writing is private, unless anyone wants to hand it in – and some do, so give them the option. This can be helpful for your own feedback and evaluation.

WHEN FURNITURE-SHIFTING ISN'T FEASIBLE

Time-panic does not sit well with meditation and stillness, so doing what is manageable is better than trying to do too much and losing the group. It just may not be feasible or possible to change your classroom by moving anything – including pupils. That doesn't mean you can't use the process. Creating ambience is basically only about facilitating a quality of *being*. So even with no furniture-shifting at all, calmness and a lowered voice can assist in this.

A background of natural sounds – the sea, a gentle brook, distant birds – muffles out any daily school-life noises. Music with a beat, or with words, is not something that I would use in this kind of prayer-context, because, it is intrudes too strongly into personal rhythms and personal words.

POSTURE

For the actual prayer-visualisation, older pupils seated on a chair, or using a prayer-stool, are usually able to assume the traditional upright posture. Alert yet relaxed. Spine straight, but not rigid, shoulders down.

However, with junior-cycle students, or those awkward about closing their eyes 'in public', leaning forward onto their desks, arms and head resting on a rolled-up jacket or a soft bag is easiest to begin with. It allows for focus on the text, and does not feel too unfamiliar. It also makes it possible for anyone choosing not to participate to opt out anonymously. This is always an option, the prevailing line being: *This is an invitation, not a command. If you choose not to participate, that is fine, provided you don't distract anyone else. Just rest quietly, where you are.* In over twenty years' experience I have never found more than two or three non-participants in a group, because this kind of prayer-opportunity is best offered when it arises out of pupil demand.

PRAYING THROUGH

It is likely that the idea of meditation is familiar, that some pupils' parents may be in prayer-groups, or attending yoga classes, where both relaxation and meditation are used. I always acknowledge any received wisdom pupils may want to display about relaxation, visualisation or meditation, because it alerts the rest of the group to the phenomenon as existing in their world, and it allows the speaker to name his/her own feelings or doubts, even if not posed as questions. If knowledge is confined to joining finger and thumb, and mouthing *Om,* I take it from there, and explain that there are many ways to meditate, as it is not a practice confined to any one religion. I might explain that Christianity has had a meditative tradition since the desert fathers and mothers of the third century, and that the purpose of meditation is not to turn inward and find only oneself, but to enter deeply in order to meet God within; as Yves Raguin, author of *Contemplating Now* once wrote, *God, in search of whom the contemplative sets out, is already within.*

The Scripture text is an opportunity for slow, thoughtful reading. It may or may not be totally fresh for the class. You might choose to use the text as part of a theme, prepared in other lessons, with a commentary and fuller background.

The relaxation is read slower again, pausing at each space on the page to allow the named action to take place. It is useful to let this happen in yourself as you read. Doing your own relaxation alongside, communicates your own deepening level, and matches the meditators' inner pace. Allow for long pauses where it seems appropriate, and especially where the dotted lines are. This is where we, as teacher, stand aside and let the Teacher come in.

Is it worth doing? I think so.

> *Today was one of the most spiritual experiences of my life. I found God. I used to think that people who meditated were 'whackos' but my view has changed. I would like to meditate every day.*
>
> (Donal, 15)

1

Taking That Step

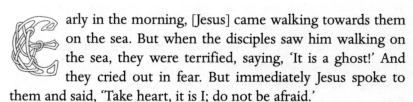 arly in the morning, [Jesus] came walking towards them on the sea. But when the disciples saw him walking on the sea, they were terrified, saying, 'It is a ghost!' And they cried out in fear. But immediately Jesus spoke to them and said, 'Take heart, it is I; do not be afraid.'

Peter answered him, 'Lord, if it is you, command me to come to you on the water.' He said, 'Come.' So Peter got out of the boat, started walking on the water, and came towards Jesus. But when he noticed the strong wind, he became frightened, and beginning to sink, he cried out, 'Lord, save me!' Jesus immediately reached out his hand and caught him, saying to him, 'You of little faith, why did you doubt?' (Matthew 14:25-33)

We now move from this passage into personal meditation,
starting off with some deep relaxation.
Whether you are sitting or lying down,
check that your body is comfortably positioned
and that you have enough space around you
to feel comfortable.
Acknowledge the fact of any sounds from inside or outside,
and then let them go...

Now, starting off by becoming aware of the points of contact
between your body and the chair or your body and the floor...
become aware of the chair or floor beneath you,
and allow it to support your body.
Relax any tightness of your tummy muscles on a slow out-breath...
warm air breathed out,
Then an in-breath, cool air breathed in,
felt on your upper lip...
Now, imagine yourself floating into warm darkness for a moment,
and allow your eyes to close.
Bring your attention down to your right foot...
Without moving the whole leg, just gently move your right ankle up and
down once or twice... then rest it again.
Still with the right foot, begin to tighten the muscles of your right calf...
and the muscles around your knee...
Hold the tension a moment or two, and then release it,
feeling that right leg relaxing and sinking.

Now, bringing your awareness to your left foot,
again gently move your ankle up and down once or twice, and then rest it.
Now just tighten the muscles of your left calf...
and the muscles around your left knee...
Hold the tension a moment or two, and then release it.
Feel the heaviness and relaxation in both legs and feet,
and check if they need to shift position at all.
If so, do so gently, and relax.

Now, on an out-breath, relax the tummy muscles around your waist...
Then let your shoulders relax by slightly lifting and then letting them
drop, or, if lying down, let them droop slightly backwards...

Now make a fist with your right hand.
Feel the tightness travel up from your wrist...
through the forearm, and upper arm, to your neck muscles...
And relax.

Now make a fist with your left hand,
again feeling the tightness in your forearm,
upper arm, neck muscles...
Again relaxing neck, shoulders, arm, wrist and hand.

With eyes still closed, slowly move your head and neck slightly,
from side to side... up and down...
until you find the most comfortable position.

Now become aware once more of your breathing,
your own ordinary breathing rhythm...
Don't force it or try to change it, just become aware of it.
Cool air breathed in, warm air breathed out... gently...
felt on your upper lip...

Now let the warm breath move aside the warm darkness, as in your
imagination, with eyes still closed, you allow yourself to enter the
meditation.

    You hear the slap of water
    against wood...
    feel the boat rocking on the tide...

    In your imagination, feel the fresh breeze
    on your face
    and the sea-salt taste on your lips...

    Like the disciples,
    you have seen Jesus approach,
    you have heard his reassurance...
    'It is I'.
    Who is Jesus – for you?

Now you watch Peter
checking... testing...
Jesus?... himself?...
You watch it happening...
the risk... the stepping over the side of the boat...
the rush and depth of water...
He is safe.

And you?
What is important now
is your *own* next step...

your own risk...
You know what you have in mind...
What is the thing that is stopping you?
It is a bit like stepping out onto the water...

Like Peter, this is your decision.
It may work...
or it may not...
You will only know if you try.

It may be big...
or small...

It is important to you.
That is what matters.

You look at Jesus...
He is still there...
The boat and where you are
seem very secure
and safe...
and it is easier to stay on board.

❧ But you know you want to follow Peter
and take that first step...
into new water.

❧ You find yourself saying this to Jesus.
He answers...
You stand up,
ready to go...
❧ You step out.
You know what this means...

❧ You look up...
the hand is there...
you are not alone.

❧ Stay with this...

And now,
slowly begin to withdraw from the scene...
Begin to be aware of your body again,
slowly moving fingers...
toes...
Gently roll your head from side to side.
Take a deep breath,
and when you are ready,
slowly open your eyes, but just looking with soft eyes...

until you are ready to move out from this space,
for now.

2

Self-Image; Who Am I?

n the third day there was a wedding in Cana of Galilee, and the mother of Jesus was there. Jesus and his disciples had also been invited to the wedding. When the wine gave out, the mother of Jesus said to him, 'They have no wine.' And Jesus said to her, 'Woman, what concern is that to you and to me? My hour has not yet come.' His mother said to the servants, 'Do whatever he tells you.' Now standing there were six stone water jars ... each holding twenty or thirty gallons. Jesus said... 'Fill the jars with water.' And they filled them up to the brim. He said to them, 'Now draw some out, and take it to the chief steward.' So they took it. When the steward tasted the water that had become wine, and did not know where it came from (though the servants who had drawn the water knew), the steward called the bridegroom and said to him, "Everyone seves the good wine first, and then the inferior wine after the guests have become drunk. But you have kept the good wine until now."' (John 2:1-9)

We now move from this passage into personal meditation,
starting off with some deep relaxation.
Whether you are sitting or lying down,
check that your body is comfortably positioned

*and that you have enough space around you
to feel comfortable.
Acknowledge the fact of any sounds from inside or outside,
and then let them go...
Now, starting off by becoming aware of the points of contact
between your body and the chair or your body and the floor...
become aware of the chair or floor beneath you,
and allow it to support your body.
Relax any tightness of your tummy muscles on a slow out-breath...
warm air breathed out,
Then an in-breath, cool air breathed in,
felt on your upper lip...
Now, imagine yourself floating into warm darkness for a moment,
and allow your eyes to close.
Bring your attention down to your right foot...
Without moving the whole leg, just gently move your right ankle up and
down once or twice... then rest it again.
Still with the right foot, begin to tighten the muscles of your right calf...
and the muscles around your knee...
Hold the tension a moment or two, and then release it,
feeling that right leg relaxing and sinking.*

*Now, bringing your awareness to your left foot,
again gently move your ankle up and down once or twice, and then rest it.
Now just tighten the muscles of your left calf...
and the muscles around your left knee...
Hold the tension a moment or two, and then release it.
Feel the heaviness and relaxation in both legs and feet,
and check if they need to shift position at all.
If so, do so gently, and relax.*

*Now, on an out-breath, relax the tummy muscles around your waist...
Then let your shoulders relax by slightly lifting and then letting them
drop, or, if lying down, let them droop slightly backwards...*

Now make a fist with your right hand.
Feel the tightness travel up from your wrist...
through the forearm, and upper arm, to your neck muscles...
And relax.
Now make a fist with your left hand,
again feeling the tightness in your forearm,
upper arm, neck muscles...
Again relaxing neck, shoulders, arm, wrist and hand.

With eyes still closed, slowly move your head and neck slightly,
from side to side... up and down...
until you find the most comfortable position.

Now become aware once more of your breathing,
your own ordinary breathing rhythm...
Don't force it or try to change it, just become aware of it.
Cool air breathed in, warm air breathed out... gently...
felt on your upper lip...

Now let the warm breath move aside the warm darkness, as in your
imagination, with eyes still closed, you allow yourself to enter the
meditation.

> In your imagination, you find yourself at the
> wedding reception.
> So, allow yourself to enter the scene...
> where it is happening, what time it is...
> indoors or outdoors...
> the size of the space, big or small,
> the number of people...

> As you look around, you begin to notice those
> water jars...
> where they are... their size...

their shape... what they are made of...
Continuing to look at them...
you now imagine yourself becoming one of them...
your own substance changing...
re-forming...
taking on the dimensions and colour
of a water jar...

As a water jar, notice the unique features of your
design...
colour, shape, beauty...
How do you feel about this?

You may also become aware
of any scratches, chips or breaks...
How do you feel about these?

Now let your awareness move to your inner sense,
and what you feel inside, as a jar.
A sense of clear space?
receptive emptiness?
hollow emptiness?

Or alternatively
a sense of fullness?
already over-filled?
cluttered?

Become aware of where you are in relation to any
other jars...
their contents changed and how you feel about this.

Do you want anything changed?
Maybe how you are is just as you want it.
You just want to say thanks

for the kind of jar you are…
But if yes,
you do want to be further changed in some way…
What way?

Jesus is there nearby,
dressed as you imagine him to be dressed…
looking as you imagine him to look…
inviting you to tell him more…

There is no hurry…
Jesus can wait…
Your time is his right time.
Take your time with him…

Stay with this…

And now,
slowly begin to withdraw from the scene…
Begin to be aware of your human body again,
slowly moving fingers…
toes…
Gently roll your head from side to side.
Take a deep breath,
and when you are ready,
slowly open your eyes, but just looking with soft eyes…

until you are ready to move out from this space,
for now.

3

Coming Alive Again

ome people came from the leader's house to say, 'Your daughter is dead. Why trouble the teacher any further?' But overhearing what they said, Jesus said to the leader of the synagogue, 'Do not fear, only believe.' ... When they came to the house of the leader of the synagogue, he saw a commotion, people weeping and wailing loudly. When he had entered, he said to them, 'Why do you make a commotion and weep? The child is not dead but sleeping.' And they laughed at him. Then he put them all outside, and took the child's father and mother and those who were with him, and went in where the child was. He took her by the hand and said to her, 'Talitha cum,' which means, 'Little girl, get up!' And immediately the girl got up and began to walk about... (Mark 5:35-36, 38-42)

We now move from this passage into personal meditation,
starting off with some deep relaxation.
Whether you are sitting or lying down,
check that your body is comfortably positioned
and that you have enough space around you
to feel comfortable.
Acknowledge the fact of any sounds from inside or outside,

and then let them go...
Now, starting off by becoming aware of the points of contact
between your body and the chair or your body and the floor...
become aware of the chair or floor beneath you,
and allow it to support your body.
Relax any tightness of your tummy muscles on a slow out-breath...
warm air breathed out,
Then an in-breath, cool air breathed in,
felt on your upper lip...
Now, imagine yourself floating into warm darkness for a moment,
and allow your eyes to close.
Bring your attention down to your right foot...
Without moving the whole leg, just gently move your right ankle up and
down once or twice... then rest it again.
Still with the right foot, begin to tighten the muscles of your right calf...
and the muscles around your knee...
Hold the tension a moment or two, and then release it,
feeling that right leg relaxing and sinking.

Now, bringing your awareness to your left foot,
again gently move your ankle up and down once or twice, and then rest it.
Now just tighten the muscles of your left calf...
and the muscles around your left knee...
Hold the tension a moment or two, and then release it.
Feel the heaviness and relaxation in both legs and feet,
and check if they need to shift position at all.
If so, do so gently, and relax.

Now, on an out-breath, relax the tummy muscles around your waist...
Then let your shoulders relax by slightly lifting and then letting them
drop, or, if lying down, let them droop slightly backwards...

Now make a fist with your right hand.
Feel the tightness travel up from your wrist...
through the forearm, and upper arm, to your neck muscles...

And relax.
Now make a fist with your left hand,
again feeling the tightness in your forearm,
upper arm, neck muscles...
Again relaxing neck, shoulders, arm, wrist and hand.

With eyes still closed, slowly move your head and neck slightly,
from side to side... up and down...
until you find the most comfortable position.

Now become aware once more of your breathing,
your own ordinary breathing rhythm...
Don't force it or try to change it, just become aware of it.
Cool air breathed in, warm air breathed out... gently...
felt on your upper lip...

Now let the warm breath move aside the warm darkness, as in your
imagination, with eyes still closed, you allow yourself to enter the
meditation.

I have been lying here for some time
in this cool room
with the pale light...

I know that inside I am still alive.
I remember
how it feels to be playful,
how to be funny and have fun...

As I lie here, gently covered with the sheet,
I remember the really good times...
where we played...
what we were at... and when...
The memories come back.

My first 'best-friend'…
my first special present…
my favourite clothes…

The good things people said about me,
family…
relatives…
even teachers…
The things I really liked about me…

The way I felt about life…
about the Lord…

But now,
I just seem to be here
lifeless…

And yet,
is that really true?
Am I really so dead…
or is it just a part of me…
at the moment?

Only a moment,
even if it has been a long moment…
How could that happen?

I hear a movement…
The door to this place is gently opening,
it was never locked…
Whose voices do I hear?

And the voice of Jesus.
He comes over…

Love, concern.
What does he want to say about my life up to now?
about the piece that feels lost...
about what feels dead...

But also about what is alive...
What does he want to say about the future?

We spend some time
listening to each other...
He understands...

He tells me he wants me to live...
all of me...
He tells me
others want me to live.
They want that inner part of me to live again.
Do I want that too?

Perhaps it is possible now
to reach out for life again...
I keep my eyes closed,
but I sense the Lord's hand
reaching for mine...
safely...

He said I was 'only sleeping'
How nice!
I can be woken...

I allow my hand to be taken.

Stay with this...

And now,
slowly begin to withdraw from the scene...
Begin to be aware of your body again,
slowly moving fingers...
toes...
Gently roll your head from side to side.
Take a deep breath,
and when you are ready,
slowly open your eyes, but just looking with soft eyes...

until you are ready to move out from this space,
for now.

4

Can I Help?

esus went up the mountain amd sat down there with his disciples... When he looked up and saw a large crowd coming toward him, Jesus said to Philip, 'Where are we to buy bread for these people to eat?' ... Philip answered him, 'Six months' wages would not buy enough bread for each of them to get a little.' One of his disciples, Andrew, Simon Peter's brother, said to him, 'There is a boy here who has five barley loaves and two fish. But what are they among so many people?' Jesus said, 'Make the people sit down.' Now there was a great deal of grass in the place; so they sat down, about five thousand in all. Then Jesus took the loaves, and when he had given thanks, he distributed them to those who were seated; so also the fish, as much as they wanted. (John 6:3-11)

We now move from this passage into personal meditation,
starting off with some deep relaxation.
Whether you are sitting or lying down,
check that your body is comfortably positioned
and that you have enough space around you
to feel comfortable.
Acknowledge the fact of any sounds from inside or outside,

and then let them go...
Now, starting off by becoming aware of the points of contact
between your body and the chair or your body and the floor...
become aware of the chair or floor beneath you,
and allow it to support your body.
Relax any tightness of your tummy muscles on a slow out-breath...
warm air breathed out,
Then an in-breath, cool air breathed in,
felt on your upper lip...
Now, imagine yourself floating into warm darkness for a moment,
and allow your eyes to close.
Bring your attention down to your right foot...
Without moving the whole leg, just gently move your right ankle up and
down once or twice... then rest it again.
Still with the right foot, begin to tighten the muscles of your right calf...
and the muscles around your knee...
Hold the tension a moment or two, and then release it,
feeling that right leg relaxing and sinking.

Now, bringing your awareness to your left foot,
again gently move your ankle up and down once or twice, and then rest it.
Now just tighten the muscles of your left calf...
and the muscles around your left knee...
Hold the tension a moment or two, and then release it.
Feel the heaviness and relaxation in both legs and feet,
and check if they need to shift position at all.
If so, do so gently, and relax.

Now, on an out-breath, relax the tummy muscles around your waist...
Then let your shoulders relax by slightly lifting and then letting them
drop, or, if lying down, let them droop slightly backwards...

Now make a fist with your right hand.
Feel the tightness travel up from your wrist...
through the forearm, and upper arm, to your neck muscles...

And relax.
Now make a fist with your left hand,
again feeling the tightness in your forearm,
upper arm, neck muscles...
Again relaxing neck, shoulders, arm, wrist and hand.

With eyes still closed, slowly move your head and neck slightly,
from side to side... up and down...
until you find the most comfortable position.

Now become aware once more of your breathing,
your own ordinary breathing rhythm...
Don't force it or try to change it, just become aware of it.
Cool air breathed in, warm air breathed out... gently...
felt on your upper lip...

Now let the warm breath move aside the warm darkness, as in your
imagination, with eyes still closed, you allow yourself to enter the
meditation.

Become aware of the wide slope of grass ahead...
its spring greenness...
and all the people sitting about...
Allow them to be familiar friends or relatives...

Because...
here among all the people
is someone who is particularly special to you...
Someone who may outside be doing fine,
but in some way you know or sense is 'hungry'.
Bring this person to mind...
Someone you care about,
someone you want to be there for...

whom you want Jesus to be there for,
as you bring the situation before him.

And, like the boy with the loaves and fishes,
you come as you are,
with what you have, to Jesus…

Jesus is here.
As with the loaves and fishes,
you ask him to make it more…

You know he shares your concern.
What is it you want to say?
Take your time…

Trusting that in some way
this person will experience your care
through Jesus…
as well as perhaps directly…

Stay with the Lord now,
both you and him
together…

And now,
slowly begin to withdraw from the scene…
Begin to be aware of your body again,
slowly moving fingers…
toes…
Gently roll your head from side to side.
Take a deep breath,
and when you are ready,
slowly open your eyes, but just looking with soft eyes…

until you are ready to move out from this space,
for now.

5

Storms

hen evening had come, [Jesus] said to [his disciples], 'Let us go across to the other side [of the lake].' And leaving the crowd behind, they took him with them in the boat, just as he was. Other boats were with him. A great windstorm arose, and the waves beat into the boat, so that the boat was already being swamped. But he was in the stern, asleep on the cushion; and they woke him up and said to him, 'Teacher, do you not care that we are perishing?' He woke up and rebuked the wind, and said to the sea, 'Peace! Be still!' Then the wind ceased, and there was a dead calm. He said to them, 'Why are you afraid? Have you still no faith?' (Mark 4:35-40)

We now move from this passage into personal meditation,
starting off with some deep relaxation.
Whether you are sitting or lying down,
check that your body is comfortably positioned
and that you have enough space around you
to feel comfortable.
Acknowledge the fact of any sounds from inside or outside,
and then let them go…
Now, starting off by becoming aware of the points of contact

between your body and the chair or your body and the floor...
become aware of the chair or floor beneath you,
and allow it to support your body.
Relax any tightness of your tummy muscles on a slow out-breath...
warm air breathed out,
Then an in-breath, cool air breathed in,
felt on your upper lip...
Now, imagine yourself floating into warm darkness for a moment,
and allow your eyes to close.
Bring your attention down to your right foot...
Without moving the whole leg, just gently move your right ankle up and
down once or twice... then rest it again.
Still with the right foot, begin to tighten the muscles of your right calf...
and the muscles around your knee...
Hold the tension a moment or two, and then release it,
feeling that right leg relaxing and sinking.

Now, bringing your awareness to your left foot,
again gently move your ankle up and down once or twice, and then rest it.
Now just tighten the muscles of your left calf...
and the muscles around your left knee...
Hold the tension a moment or two, and then release it.
Feel the heaviness and relaxation in both legs and feet,
and check if they need to shift position at all.
If so, do so gently, and relax.

Now, on an out-breath, relax the tummy muscles around your waist...
Then let your shoulders relax by slightly lifting and then letting them
drop, or, if lying down, let them droop slightly backwards...

Now make a fist with your right hand.
Feel the tightness travel up from your wrist...
through the forearm, and upper arm, to your neck muscles...
And relax.
Now make a fist with your left hand,

again feeling the tightness in your forearm,
upper arm, neck muscles…
Again relaxing neck, shoulders, arm, wrist and hand.

With eyes still closed, slowly move your head and neck slightly,
from side to side… up and down…
until you find the most comfortable position.

Now become aware once more of your breathing,
your own ordinary breathing rhythm…
Don't force it or try to change it, just become aware of it.
Cool air breathed in, warm air breathed out… gently…
felt on your upper lip…

Now let the warm breath move aside the warm darkness, as in your
imagination, with eyes still closed, you allow yourself to enter the
meditation.

 Somehow you find yourself on this boat
willing…
or reluctant…
Where is it heading?
Where has it started from?
How long have you been out here?

It seems the boat is tossing…
Your friends are busy with their own concerns,
or even asleep.

It all seems too confusing…
or dark…
upside down…

Become aware of the size of the waves,
and the sounds that come with the storm.
The water swells high, pouring over everything,
overwhelming.

But where is the storm centred?
Is there any part of it inside?

Where?
What is it about?
Does this storm have words,
as well as confusion?

Why, why?
Resentment?
Anger?

And…
'Don't you care?' you hear the others say to Jesus.
What would you want to say?

Is this a question for the Lord?

Actually, Jesus is not asleep now.
He is prepared to invite you over…
If you want…
And when you want…

How does that feel?
What can he see of your storm?
He seems to know…
He does hear you…
He stands up and faces your storm…

Together you face it…

If and when you feel ready,
if and when it feels appropriate,
breathe quietly in,
on a deep breath...
and again...
receive whatever he wants to offer...
Wherever you feel yourself to be,
be there, not alone, but with the Lord now.

You may find you hear those words,
'Be still.'
If not now,
then as a promise...
With hope.

Stay with this...

And now,
slowly begin to withdraw from the scene...
Begin to be aware of your body again,
slowly moving fingers...
toes...
Gently roll your head from side to side.
Take a deep breath,
and when you are ready,
slowly open your eyes, but just looking with soft eyes...

until you are ready to move out from this space,
for now.

6

Feeling Stuck

n Jerusalem, by the Sheep Gate there is a pool, called in Hebrew Beth-zatha, which has five porticoes. In these lay many invalids – blind, lame, and paralyzed. One man was there who had been ill for thirty-eight years. When Jesus saw him lying there and knew that he had been there a long time, he said to him, 'Do you want to be made well?' The sick man answered him, 'Sir, I have no one to put me into the pool when the water is stirred up; and while I am making my way, someone else steps down ahead of me.' Jesus said to him, 'Stand up, take your mat and walk.' (John 5:2-8)

We now move from this passage into personal meditation,
starting off with some deep relaxation.
Whether you are sitting or lying down,
check that your body is comfortably positioned
and that you have enough space around you
to feel comfortable.
Acknowledge the fact of any sounds from inside or outside,
and then let them go…
Now, starting off by becoming aware of the points of contact
between your body and the chair or your body and the floor…

become aware of the chair or floor beneath you,
and allow it to support your body.
Relax any tightness of your tummy muscles on a slow out-breath...
warm air breathed out,
Then an in-breath, cool air breathed in,
felt on your upper lip...
Now, imagine yourself floating into warm darkness for a moment,
and allow your eyes to close.
Bring your attention down to your right foot...
Without moving the whole leg, just gently move your right ankle up and
down once or twice... then rest it again.
Still with the right foot, begin to tighten the muscles of your right calf...
and the muscles around your knee...
Hold the tension a moment or two, and then release it,
feeling that right leg relaxing and sinking.

Now, bringing your awareness to your left foot,
again gently move your ankle up and down once or twice, and then rest it.
Now just tighten the muscles of your left calf...
and the muscles around your left knee...
Hold the tension a moment or two, and then release it.
Feel the heaviness and relaxation in both legs and feet,
and check if they need to shift position at all.
If so, do so gently, and relax.

Now, on an out-breath, relax the tummy muscles around your waist...
Then let your shoulders relax by slightly lifting and then letting them
drop, or, if lying down, let them droop slightly backwards...

Now make a fist with your right hand.
Feel the tightness travel up from your wrist...
through the forearm, and upper arm, to your neck muscles...
And relax.
Now make a fist with your left hand,
again feeling the tightness in your forearm,

upper arm, neck muscles...
Again relaxing neck, shoulders, arm, wrist and hand.

With eyes still closed, slowly move your head and neck slightly,
from side to side... up and down...
until you find the most comfortable position.

Now become aware once more of your breathing,
your own ordinary breathing rhythm...
Don't force it or try to change it, just become aware of it.
Cool air breathed in, warm air breathed out... gently...
felt on your upper lip...

Now let the warm breath move aside the warm darkness, as in your
imagination, with eyes still closed, you allow yourself to enter the
meditation.

There on the roofed porch, alongside all the others,
you have your own little space...
a bit cut off...
You know what it looks like,
how big...
or how small it is...
and how near...
or far...
from the opportunity for healing.

You try, you really have tried,
and it is always the same.
It never works out...
Others who want what you want
always get there before you...

Stay with these thoughts a moment...
What is it you would want to do or be
if you didn't feel so helpless?...

What is in the gap between wanting and doing?
Are you allowing something – or someone –
to actually hold you down ...
keep you feeling so paralysed?

Is it your own fear,
insecurity?
Is this something you can begin to talk to the Lord
about?
Even if you don't expect it to change overnight?

Yet as you see the paralysed man walk away,
perhaps there is a part of you
that hopes things might be different for you too,

even a little bit different
from how it has been...
for so long.

Jesus is actually there for you.
How does trust begin?
Being real in the present moment?
Knowing he knows all the past, as you do?
Ask him.

He won't change you being you,
with all your life and history,
but he can strengthen you.
He can show you how to stand up
stronger...

using all your less-known strengths.
You think of what these might be...
with his.

He invites you to focus on those strengths,
the part or parts of yourself
that feel held back...
To name the feeling that keeps you here...
to name it and then hand that feeling over to him...

Now he invites you
to welcome the part of yourself
that wants to get up
and move on...

The part
perhaps hidden up to now,
that is strong –
at least in desire...

You notice
he is offering you his hand...
Somehow you know that taking it
will be the beginning...
You reach out.
You breathe deeply
for a moment or two...
Become aware of the original place
of feeling stuck
and have a sense of this now...
Is there any loosening
of the paralysis?
If not,
you simply wait with the Lord,
knowing healing is a process...

Let it take its time.
And if you do feel some inner movement,
then, in your imagination,
You can try standing,
 test out a new strength,
hope to take a first step...

 Stay with this...

And now,
slowly begin to withdraw from the scene...
Begin to be aware of your body again,
slowly moving fingers...
toes...
Gently roll your head from side to side.
Take a deep breath,
and when you are ready,
slowly open your eyes, but just looking with soft eyes...

until you are ready to move out from this space,
for now.

7

Trusting the Future

o not let your hearts be troubled. Believe in God, believe also in me. In my Father's house there are many dwelling places. If it were not so, would I have told you that I go to prepare a place for you? And if I go to prepare a place for you, I will come again and will take you to myself, so that where I am, there you may be also. And you know the way to the place where I am going. Thomas said to him, 'Lord, we do not know where you are going. How can we know the way?' Jesus said to him, 'I am the way, and the truth, and the life. No one comes to the Father except through me. If you know me, you will know my Father also. From now on you do know him and have seen him. (John 14:1-7)

We now move from this passage into personal meditation,
starting off with some deep relaxation.
Whether you are sitting or lying down,
check that your body is comfortably positioned
and that you have enough space around you
to feel comfortable.
Acknowledge the fact of any sounds from inside or outside,
and then let them go…

*Now, starting off by becoming aware of the points of contact
between your body and the chair or your body and the floor…
become aware of the chair or floor beneath you,
and allow it to support your body.
Relax any tightness of your tummy muscles on a slow out-breath…
warm air breathed out,
Then an in-breath, cool air breathed in,
felt on your upper lip…
Now, imagine yourself floating into warm darkness for a moment,
and allow your eyes to close.
Bring your attention down to your right foot…
Without moving the whole leg, just gently move your right ankle up and
down once or twice… then rest it again.
Still with the right foot, begin to tighten the muscles of your right calf…
and the muscles around your knee…
Hold the tension a moment or two, and then release it,
feeling that right leg relaxing and sinking.*

*Now, bringing your awareness to your left foot,
again gently move your ankle up and down once or twice, and then rest it.
Now just tighten the muscles of your left calf…
and the muscles around your left knee…
Hold the tension a moment or two, and then release it.
Feel the heaviness and relaxation in both legs and feet,
and check if they need to shift position at all.
If so, do so gently, and relax.*

*Now, on an out-breath, relax the tummy muscles around your waist…
Then let your shoulders relax by slightly lifting and then letting them
drop, or, if lying down, let them droop slightly backwards…*

*Now make a fist with your right hand.
Feel the tightness travel up from your wrist…
through the forearm, and upper arm, to your neck muscles…
And relax.*

Now make a fist with your left hand,
again feeling the tightness in your forearm,
upper arm, neck muscles...
Again relaxing neck, shoulders, arm, wrist and hand.

With eyes still closed, slowly move your head and neck slightly,
from side to side... up and down...
until you find the most comfortable position.

Now become aware once more of your breathing,
your own ordinary breathing rhythm...
Don't force it or try to change it, just become aware of it.
Cool air breathed in, warm air breathed out... gently...
felt on your upper lip...

Now let the warm breath move aside the warm darkness, as in your
imagination, with eyes still closed, you allow yourself to enter the
meditation.

This passage from the Last Supper
is read a second time,
slowly, phrase by phrase.

You listen for any phrase
or sentence
that particularly speaks to you
in your present experience.
You stay with that sentence or phrase,
and let it become Jesus' word in you.
You let other passing words and phrases go.
When a new one is needed, it will be there.
One phrase may be enough.
Perhaps you may use it later with your breathing –
taking a half on an in-breath and

half on an out-breath.

 Perhaps you might like to hold an image of Jesus in
your imagination,
as you hear the words being spoken.
This could be by sitting near him at the Last Supper
where these words were spoken.
 But you follow what comes...
as you place yourself in his presence.

The Scripture text is re-read. Savour the words and allow for the pauses...

And now,
slowly begin to withdraw from the scene...
Begin to be aware of your body again,
slowly moving fingers...
toes...
Gently roll your head from side to side.
Take a deep breath,
and when you are ready,
slowly open your eyes, but just looking with soft eyes...

until you are ready to move out from this space,
for now.

8

Sorry

h e [Jesus] saw two boats there at the shore of the lake; the fishermen had gone out of them and were washing their nets. He got into one of the boats, the one belonging to Simon, and asked him to put out a little way from the shore. Then he sat down and taught the crowds from the boat. When he had finished speaking, he said to Simon, 'Put out into the deep water and let down your nets for a catch.' Simon answered, 'Master, we have worked all night long, but have caught nothing. Yet if you say so, I will let down the nets.' When they had done this, they caught so many fish that their nets were beginning to break. So they signaled their partners in the other boat to come and help them. And they came and filled both boats, so that they began to sink. But when Simon Peter saw it, he fell down at Jesus' knees, saying, 'Go away from me, Lord, for I am a sinful man!' (Luke 5:2-8)

We now move from this passage into personal meditation,
starting off with some deep relaxation.
Whether you are sitting or lying down,
check that your body is comfortably positioned
and that you have enough space around you
to feel comfortable.

Acknowledge the fact of any sounds from inside or outside,
and then let them go…
Now, starting off by becoming aware of the points of contact
between your body and the chair or your body and the floor…
become aware of the chair or floor beneath you,
and allow it to support your body.
Relax any tightness of your tummy muscles on a slow out-breath…
warm air breathed out,
Then an in-breath, cool air breathed in,
felt on your upper lip…
Now, imagine yourself floating into warm darkness for a moment,
and allow your eyes to close.
Bring your attention down to your right foot…
Without moving the whole leg, just gently move your right ankle up and
down once or twice… then rest it again.
Still with the right foot, begin to tighten the muscles of your right calf…
and the muscles around your knee…
Hold the tension a moment or two, and then release it,
feeling that right leg relaxing and sinking.

Now, bringing your awareness to your left foot,
again gently move your ankle up and down once or twice, and then rest it.
Now just tighten the muscles of your left calf…
and the muscles around your left knee…
Hold the tension a moment or two, and then release it.
Feel the heaviness and relaxation in both legs and feet,
and check if they need to shift position at all.
If so, do so gently, and relax.

Now, on an out-breath, relax the tummy muscles around your waist…
Then let your shoulders relax by slightly lifting and then letting them
drop, or, if lying down, let them droop slightly backwards…

Now make a fist with your right hand.
Feel the tightness travel up from your wrist…

through the forearm, and upper arm, to your neck muscles...
And relax.
Now make a fist with your left hand,
again feeling the tightness in your forearm,
upper arm, neck muscles...
Again relaxing neck, shoulders, arm, wrist and hand.

With eyes still closed, slowly move your head and neck slightly,
from side to side... up and down...
until you find the most comfortable position.

Now become aware once more of your breathing,
your own ordinary breathing rhythm...
Don't force it or try to change it, just become aware of it.
Cool air breathed in, warm air breathed out... gently...
felt on your upper lip...

Now let the warm breath move aside the warm darkness, as in your
imagination, with eyes still closed, you allow yourself to enter the
meditation.

You see the nets wet and heavy,
the boats riding low in the water,
and activity all around...
You're there,
observing, allowing yourself to be drawn in...
Amidst all the activity,
you notice something.

Over there, just to the side,
Jesus and Peter...
You are just in time to hear Peter saying,
'Go away from me...'
Does he mean that?
Jesus has just shown how interested he is in his life

and work…
And now, 'Go away?'

What has shut him down?
Something he is uncomfortable with?
Wants to get away from?
He uses the word 'sin'.
Does he mean the ways he has done wrong?
The ways he perhaps betrayed himself?
In word or action?

Jesus is calm.
He doesn't agree or disagree.
He lets Peter say, confess,
what he needs to.
And he stays with Peter.

The future isn't finished
because of the past.
In fact, he tells Peter of
a new approach to doing his job.
Same job, new perspective.

You reflect on yourself,
on what parts of your life
would make you want to say
'Go away'…

Peter looks at you.
His unspoken question,
'Are you like me?
Are there aspects of your life that
you want to disown?
Things that you do or did
that you could do without?'

And he seems to say
Where can you go?
You reflect on this...
You saw Jesus accepting Peter,
not judging,
not condemning,
but not denying either.

Can you believe that Jesus can accept all of you?
the best you...
the confused you...
the 'still-in-process' you?

Peter believes
in his heart
that Jesus has forgiven him.
The question is,
can *you* accept that forgiveness?
Can you forgive *yourself*?

Jesus is there...
You have the choice...
If it feels appropriate
and if you feel ready...
Take the space that Peter took,
and sit with Jesus...

Stay with this...

And now,
slowly begin to withdraw from the scene...
Begin to be aware of your body again,
slowly moving fingers...
toes...

Gently roll your head from side to side.
Take a deep breath,
and when you are ready,
slowly open your eyes, but just looking with soft eyes…

until you are ready to move out from this space,
for now.

9

Difficult Choices

s [Jesus] and his disciples and a large crowd were leaving
Jericho, Bartimaeus, son of Timaeus, a blind beggar, was
sitting by the roadside. When he heard that it was Jesus of
Nazareth, he began to shout out and say, 'Jesus, Son of
David, have mercy on me!' Many sternly ordered him to be quiet,
but he cried out even more loudly, 'Son of David, have mercy on
me!' Jesus stood still and said, 'Call him here.' And they called the
blind man, saying to him, 'Take heart; get up, he is calling you.' So
throwing off his cloak, he sprang up and came to Jesus. Then Jesus
said to him, 'What do you want me to do for you?' The blind man
said to him, 'My teacher, let me see again.' Jesus said to him, 'Go;
your faith has made you well.' Immediately he regained his sight
and followed him on the way. (Mark 10:46-52)

We now move from this passage into personal meditation,
starting off with some deep relaxation.
Whether you are sitting or lying down,
check that your body is comfortably positioned
and that you have enough space around you
to feel comfortable.
Acknowledge the fact of any sounds from inside or outside,

and then let them go...
Now, starting off by becoming aware of the points of contact
between your body and the chair or your body and the floor...
become aware of the chair or floor beneath you,
and allow it to support your body.
Relax any tightness of your tummy muscles on a slow out-breath...
warm air breathed out,
Then an in-breath, cool air breathed in,
felt on your upper lip...
Now, imagine yourself floating into warm darkness for a moment,
and allow your eyes to close.
Bring your attention down to your right foot...
Without moving the whole leg, just gently move your right ankle up and
down once or twice... then rest it again.
Still with the right foot, begin to tighten the muscles of your right calf...
and the muscles around your knee...
Hold the tension a moment or two, and then release it,
feeling that right leg relaxing and sinking.

Now, bringing your awareness to your left foot,
again gently move your ankle up and down once or twice, and then rest it.
Now just tighten the muscles of your left calf...
and the muscles around your left knee...
Hold the tension a moment or two, and then release it.
Feel the heaviness and relaxation in both legs and feet,
and check if they need to shift position at all.
If so, do so gently, and relax.

Now, on an out-breath, relax the tummy muscles around your waist...
Then let your shoulders relax by slightly lifting and then letting them
drop, or, if lying down, let them droop slightly backwards...

Now make a fist with your right hand.
Feel the tightness travel up from your wrist...
through the forearm, and upper arm, to your neck muscles...

And relax.
Now make a fist with your left hand,
again feeling the tightness in your forearm,
upper arm, neck muscles...
Again relaxing neck, shoulders, arm, wrist and hand.

With eyes still closed, slowly move your head and neck slightly,
from side to side... up and down...
until you find the most comfortable position.

Now become aware once more of your breathing,
your own ordinary breathing rhythm...
Don't force it or try to change it, just become aware of it.
Cool air breathed in, warm air breathed out... gently...
felt on your upper lip...

Now let the warm breath move aside the warm darkness, as in your
imagination, with eyes still closed, you allow yourself to enter the
meditation.

> I imagine myself
> sitting on the ground beside Bartimaeus...
> and hear the soft-dust shuffle of passing feet...
> hear the clink of coins being tossed...
> fragments of other people's lives passing...
>
> Bartimaeus is between two places.
> He has settled for somewhere half-way.
> And up to now he has been begging for the means
> to survive this in-between, unseeing place.
>
> Yet now there is a deeper kind of begging.
> He wants to see in order to move on...

Using the only name he knows
he calls out to Jesus, and Jesus stops...
He listens...
He waits...

Not only for Bartimaeus... for me.
Am I also between two places, two choices,
two decisions?...
A personal challenge?
a relationship?
a study-option?
a career-change?
I name it...

And in naming it,
what do I still need to make the choice?
From whom?
What is stopping me?

If I too were to call Jesus in on this,
what name would I use?
Why?
Does this name bring memories?

and when he calls me...
what name does *he* use?
The one I am most comfortable with?
Is this who I am with you, Jesus?

Like Bartimaeus, I feel I may need help
to come to this place of choosing.

I reflect on those special people who have already
helped me...
But now...

Jesus is here…
He asks the most important question,
What do you *want*?

What *do* I want?
This is the question for my heart.
I have heard the heart and energy in Bartimaeus,
expressed as begging.

What is begging in me?
What needs to be begged louder?
Where do I seek sight,
not blindness?
Where do I find life?

What cloak do I also need to throw aside?
Am I ready?
Is it now,
or is this simply
a beginning for now?

I listen…
I respond…
that I may see…

I stay with this…

And now,
slowly begin to withdraw from the scene…
Begin to be aware of your body again,
slowly moving fingers…
toes…
Gently roll your head from side to side.
Take a deep breath,

and when you are ready,
slowly open your eyes, but just looking with soft eyes...

until you are ready to move out from this space,
for now.

10

A Place in My Family

 t has been written by the prophet: 'And you, Bethlehem, in
the land of Judah, are by no means least among the rulers of
Judah; for from you shall come a ruler who is to shepherd my
people Israel.' (Matthew 2:6)

We now move from this passage into personal meditation,
starting off with some deep relaxation.
Whether you are sitting or lying down,
check that your body is comfortably positioned
and that you have enough space around you
to feel comfortable.
Acknowledge the fact of any sounds from inside or outside,
and then let them go...
Now, starting off by becoming aware of the points of contact
between your body and the chair or your body and the floor...
become aware of the chair or floor beneath you,
and allow it to support your body.
Relax any tightness of your tummy muscles on a slow out-breath...
warm air breathed out,
Then an in-breath, cool air breathed in,
felt on your upper lip...

Now, imagine yourself floating into warm darkness for a moment,
and allow your eyes to close.
Bring your attention down to your right foot...
Without moving the whole leg, just gently move your right ankle up and
down once or twice... then rest it again.
Still with the right foot, begin to tighten the muscles of your right calf...
and the muscles around your knee...
Hold the tension a moment or two, and then release it,
feeling that right leg relaxing and sinking.

Now, bringing your awareness to your left foot,
again gently move your ankle up and down once or twice, and then rest it.
Now just tighten the muscles of your left calf...
and the muscles around your left knee...
Hold the tension a moment or two, and then release it.
Feel the heaviness and relaxation in both legs and feet,
and check if they need to shift position at all.
If so, do so gently, and relax.

Now, on an out-breath, relax the tummy muscles around your waist...
Then let your shoulders relax by slightly lifting and then letting them
drop, or, if lying down, let them droop slightly backwards...

Now make a fist with your right hand.
Feel the tightness travel up from your wrist...
through the forearm, and upper arm, to your neck muscles...
And relax.
Now make a fist with your left hand,
again feeling the tightness in your forearm,
upper arm, neck muscles...
Again relaxing neck, shoulders, arm, wrist and hand.

With eyes still closed, slowly move your head and neck slightly,
from side to side... up and down...
until you find the most comfortable position.

Now become aware once more of your breathing,
your own ordinary breathing rhythm...
Don't force it or try to change it, just become aware of it.
Cool air breathed in, warm air breathed out... gently...
felt on your upper lip...

Now let the warm breath move aside the warm darkness, as in your
imagination, with eyes still closed, you allow yourself to enter the
meditation.

In your imagination, picture a family photograph,
either real, or imaginary,
with you in it ...
Settle the date and place...

Look at the members of your family...
naming each...
seeing them in their own special pose.

Now choose someone from the picture
whom you want to bring with you into this
meditation...

Is this person still alive?
Or is it memories that will bring them alive for you at
this time?

In imagination, bring to mind any memories
or family stories about this person
that make you glad that you belong with them...

Experience your gladness for anything in particular.
And rest with this for a few moments.

Now, if you wish,
do the same with
any other person in the picture,
or anyone you think should be in the picture.

Remembering
features, shape, qualities,
whatever it is that makes them real for you...
holding gratitude as prayer.

And so on, meeting as many as feels right at this
time...

Then, if you wish,
allow your mind to move gently over the past,
and see if you can remember
any moment that gave you
a sense of being supported by your family...
See if you can recall that experience now,
and the comfort and care it gave you...

Allow yourself to bring any particularly good
moments to mind...

Be there again...
Feel the sense of belonging,
of being part of a family
for what this means...

Perhaps needing to acknowledge
it isn't always good...
not always happy...

but for what was,
and still is...

❧   for what you've learned...
       and grown through...
       Give thanks.

❧   Stay with this...

And now,
slowly begin to withdraw from the scene...
Begin to be aware of your body again,
slowly moving fingers...
toes...
Gently roll your head from side to side.
Take a deep breath,
and when you are ready,
slowly open your eyes, but just looking with soft eyes...

until you are ready to move out from this space,
for now.

11

Following Your Inner Star

hen Herod secretly called for the wise men and learned from them the exact time when the star had appeared... When they had heard the king they set out; and there, ahead of them, went the star that they had seen at its rising, until it stopped over the place where the child was. When they saw that the star had stopped, they were overwhelmed with joy. On entering the house, they saw the child with Mary his mother; and they knelt down and paid him homage. Then, opening their treasure chests, they offered him gifts of gold, frankincense and myrrh. (Matthew 2:7-11)

We now move from this passage into personal meditation,
starting off with some deep relaxation.
Whether you are sitting or lying down,
check that your body is comfortably positioned
and that you have enough space around you
to feel comfortable.
Acknowledge the fact of any sounds from inside or outside,
and then let them go...
Now, starting off by becoming aware of the points of contact
between your body and the chair or your body and the floor...

become aware of the chair or floor beneath you,
and allow it to support your body.
Relax any tightness of your tummy muscles on a slow out-breath...
warm air breathed out,
Then an in-breath, cool air breathed in,
felt on your upper lip...
Now, imagine yourself floating into warm darkness for a moment,
and allow your eyes to close.
Bring your attention down to your right foot...
Without moving the whole leg, just gently move your right ankle up and
down once or twice... then rest it again.
Still with the right foot, begin to tighten the muscles of your right calf...
and the muscles around your knee...
Hold the tension a moment or two, and then release it,
feeling that right leg relaxing and sinking.

Now, bringing your awareness to your left foot,
again gently move your ankle up and down once or twice, and then rest it.
Now just tighten the muscles of your left calf...
and the muscles around your left knee...
Hold the tension a moment or two, and then release it.
Feel the heaviness and relaxation in both legs and feet,
and check if they need to shift position at all.
If so, do so gently, and relax.

Now, on an out-breath, relax the tummy muscles around your waist...
Then let your shoulders relax by slightly lifting and then letting them
drop, or, if lying down, let them droop slightly backwards...

Now make a fist with your right hand.
Feel the tightness travel up from your wrist...
through the forearm, and upper arm, to your neck muscles...
And relax.
Now make a fist with your left hand,
again feeling the tightness in your forearm,

upper arm, neck muscles...
Again relaxing neck, shoulders, arm, wrist and hand.

With eyes still closed, slowly move your head and neck slightly,
from side to side... up and down...
until you find the most comfortable position.

Now become aware once more of your breathing,
your own ordinary breathing rhythm...
Don't force it or try to change it, just become aware of it.
Cool air breathed in, warm air breathed out... gently...
felt on your upper lip...

Now let the warm breath move aside the warm darkness, as in your
imagination, with eyes still closed, you allow yourself to enter the
meditation.

The sound of travellers arriving at the stable...
You are among them.
Day and night
you have followed your star...
You look around...
Where have you arrived?

You see the others taking out their gifts.
You have yours, but first,
you turn aside
for a moment...
looking back at the landscape
across which you have travelled...
seeing the paths you have taken,
the places at which you felt you had arrived.

Particular incidents
or celebrations come to mind.

You remember the time
when you felt a sense of inner direction,
your inner star telling you
'This is where you must go,
This is what you must do.'

Perhaps it wasn't so clear,
simply a faint feeling of rightness...

a school to go to,
a person to talk to,
a place to be in,
a job to choose,
a call from God,

Remember the first time you ever came to know of
God...
at home?
at school?
at Mass?
through an experience of God in creation,
in mountains, the sea, flowers, beauty?

Recall that personal experience
and reflect on the significant steps
that followed from the first sighting
of your inner star until now.

Looking back
from your personal journey so far
into the present...

Where are you now?
In what circumstances
are you now recognising the Lord?
From where you have travelled,
what is the particular gift
that you can now say you received?
and which may now be the one you are able to
bring...

As you now enter the stable,
you may like to share your story with Mary.

Stay with this...

And now,
slowly begin to withdraw from the scene...
Begin to be aware of your body again,
slowly moving fingers...
toes...
Gently roll your head from side to side.
Take a deep breath,
and when you are ready,
slowly open your eyes, but just looking with soft eyes...

until you are ready to move out from this space,
for now.

12

Asking for What I Need

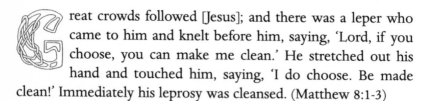reat crowds followed [Jesus]; and there was a leper who came to him and knelt before him, saying, 'Lord, if you choose, you can make me clean.' He stretched out his hand and touched him, saying, 'I do choose. Be made clean!' Immediately his leprosy was cleansed. (Matthew 8:1-3)

We now move from this passage into personal meditation,
starting off with some deep relaxation.
Whether you are sitting or lying down,
check that your body is comfortably positioned
and that you have enough space around you
to feel comfortable.
Acknowledge the fact of any sounds from inside or outside,
and then let them go...
Now, starting off by becoming aware of the points of contact
between your body and the chair or your body and the floor...
become aware of the chair or floor beneath you,
and allow it to support your body.
Relax any tightness of your tummy muscles on a slow out-breath...
warm air breathed out,
Then an in-breath, cool air breathed in,

felt on your upper lip...
Now, imagine yourself floating into warm darkness for a moment,
and allow your eyes to close.
Bring your attention down to your right foot...
Without moving the whole leg, just gently move your right ankle up and
down once or twice... then rest it again.
Still with the right foot, begin to tighten the muscles of your right calf...
and the muscles around your knee...
Hold the tension a moment or two, and then release it,
feeling that right leg relaxing and sinking.

Now, bringing your awareness to your left foot,
again gently move your ankle up and down once or twice, and then rest it.
Now just tighten the muscles of your left calf...
and the muscles around your left knee...
Hold the tension a moment or two, and then release it.
Feel the heaviness and relaxation in both legs and feet,
and check if they need to shift position at all.
If so, do so gently, and relax.

Now, on an out-breath, relax the tummy muscles around your waist...
Then let your shoulders relax by slightly lifting and then letting them
drop, or, if lying down, let them droop slightly backwards...

Now make a fist with your right hand.
Feel the tightness travel up from your wrist...
through the forearm, and upper arm, to your neck muscles...
And relax.
Now make a fist with your left hand,
again feeling the tightness in your forearm,
upper arm, neck muscles...
Again relaxing neck, shoulders, arm, wrist and hand.

With eyes still closed, slowly move your head and neck slightly,
from side to side... up and down...

until you find the most comfortable position.

Now become aware once more of your breathing,
your own ordinary breathing rhythm...
Don't force it or try to change it, just become aware of it.
Cool air breathed in, warm air breathed out... gently...
felt on your upper lip...

Now let the warm breath move aside the warm darkness, as in your
imagination, with eyes still closed, you allow yourself to enter the
meditation.

A crowded street;
people your age,
getting on with life...

You become aware
of the leper...
less because of the details of his illness
and what he looks like
than for what he says
and how he says it...

'If you want to ... you can heal me.'
The leper knows that Jesus has a choice.
He speaks from his own experience of doing
something,
because he knows that he too has a choice,
To ask
or not to bother asking?

And what to ask?
What will healing mean?

The leper knows that what he asks may not happen
as he may expect it to,
but he takes the risk
in trust.

He hears the words of warmth:
'Of course I want to.'

Healing may be
the thing you ask too.
Could you accept it if the 'Yes'
turns out different from your expectation?

Is it enough that you just ask,
and leave the outcome to the Healer?

You look at Jesus...
'Of course I want to'...
If it now feels appropriate,
dare to ask...

Stay with this...

And now,
slowly begin to withdraw from the scene...
Begin to be aware of your body again,
slowly moving fingers...
toes...
Gently roll your head from side to side.
Take a deep breath,
and when you are ready,
slowly open your eyes, but just looking with soft eyes...

until you are ready to move out from this space,
for now.

13

Me and Other People

'What must I do to inherit eternal life?' [someone asked] [Jesus] said to him, 'What is written in the law? What do you read there?' He answered, 'You shall love the Lord your God with all your heart, and with all your soul, and with all your strength, and with all your mind; and your neighbour as yourself.' And he said to him, 'You have given the right answer; do this, and you will live.' But wanting to justify himself, he asked Jesus, 'And who is my neighbour?' (Luke 10:25-29)

We now move from this passage into personal meditation,
starting off with some deep relaxation.
Whether you are sitting or lying down,
check that your body is comfortably positioned
and that you have enough space around you
to feel comfortable.
Acknowledge the fact of any sounds from inside or outside,
and then let them go…
Now, starting off by becoming aware of the points of contact
between your body and the chair or your body and the floor…
become aware of the chair or floor beneath you,
and allow it to support your body.

Relax any tightness of your tummy muscles on a slow out-breath...
warm air breathed out,
Then an in-breath, cool air breathed in,
felt on your upper lip...
Now, imagine yourself floating into warm darkness for a moment,
and allow your eyes to close.
Bring your attention down to your right foot...
Without moving the whole leg, just gently move your right ankle up and
down once or twice... then rest it again.
Still with the right foot, begin to tighten the muscles of your right calf...
and the muscles around your knee...
Hold the tension a moment or two, and then release it,
feeling that right leg relaxing and sinking.

Now, bringing your awareness to your left foot,
again gently move your ankle up and down once or twice, and then rest it.
Now just tighten the muscles of your left calf...
and the muscles around your left knee...
Hold the tension a moment or two, and then release it.
Feel the heaviness and relaxation in both legs and feet,
and check if they need to shift position at all.
If so, do so gently, and relax.

Now, on an out-breath, relax the tummy muscles around your waist...
Then let your shoulders relax by slightly lifting and then letting them
drop, or, if lying down, let them droop slightly backwards...

Now make a fist with your right hand.
Feel the tightness travel up from your wrist...
through the forearm, and upper arm, to your neck muscles...
And relax.
Now make a fist with your left hand,
again feeling the tightness in your forearm,
upper arm, neck muscles...
Again relaxing neck, shoulders, arm, wrist and hand.

With eyes still closed, slowly move your head and neck slightly,
from side to side... up and down...
until you find the most comfortable position.

Now become aware once more of your breathing,
your own ordinary breathing rhythm...
Don't force it or try to change it, just become aware of it.
Cool air breathed in, warm air breathed out... gently...
felt on your upper lip...

Now let the warm breath move aside the warm darkness, as in your
imagination, with eyes still closed, you allow yourself to enter the
meditation.

      ❧   Neighbour.
             An old-fashioned word?
             A burden even?

      ❧   Or a good word,
             meaning something?

      ❧   Neighbour.
             Where?
             At home?
             At school?
      ❧   At work?
             Same desk?
             Same class?
             Same family?
      ❧   Extended family?

             What am I supposed to do?

      ❧   Who is the real person
             that is under my skin

enough to be called 'neighbour'
– maybe also friend?

But what if this is it?
What if this neighbour is not near enough
to be called friend?

Love your neighbour?

What do I learn about myself
as I think about this person?
Am I open
or withdrawing?
Why?

What parts of me
want so much to belong only to me
...that could be
for sharing?

Love your neighbour.

Does this mean wish them well?
Greet them,
be at home in my heart
if I'm home in my house, room, school, desk, etc?

Is that it?
Just don't close the door?
Keep it open.
I see.

Love my neighbour.

Stay with this...

And now,
slowly begin to withdraw from the scene...
Begin to be aware of your body again,
slowly moving fingers...
toes...
Gently roll your head from side to side.
Take a deep breath,
and when you are ready,
slowly open your eyes, but just looking with soft eyes...

until you are ready to move out from this space,
for now.

14

I Am Heard

o I [Jesus] say to you, Ask, and it will be given you; search, and you will find; knock, and the door will be opened for you. For everyone who asks receives, and everyone who searches finds, and for everyone who knocks, the door will be opened. (Luke 11:9-10)

We now move from this passage into personal meditation,
starting off with some deep relaxation.
Whether you are sitting or lying down,
check that your body is comfortably positioned
and that you have enough space around you
to feel comfortable.
Acknowledge the fact of any sounds from inside or outside,
and then let them go…
Now, starting off by becoming aware of the points of contact
between your body and the chair or your body and the floor…
become aware of the chair or floor beneath you,
and allow it to support your body.
Relax any tightness of your tummy muscles on a slow out-breath…
warm air breathed out,
Then an in-breath, cool air breathed in,

felt on your upper lip...
Now, imagine yourself floating into warm darkness for a moment,
and allow your eyes to close.
Bring your attention down to your right foot...
Without moving the whole leg, just gently move your right ankle up and
down once or twice... then rest it again.
Still with the right foot, begin to tighten the muscles of your right calf...
and the muscles around your knee...
Hold the tension a moment or two, and then release it,
feeling that right leg relaxing and sinking.

Now, bringing your awareness to your left foot,
again gently move your ankle up and down once or twice, and then rest it.
Now just tighten the muscles of your left calf...
and the muscles around your left knee...
Hold the tension a moment or two, and then release it.
Feel the heaviness and relaxation in both legs and feet,
and check if they need to shift position at all.
If so, do so gently, and relax.

Now, on an out-breath, relax the tummy muscles around your waist...
Then let your shoulders relax by slightly lifting and then letting them
drop, or, if lying down, let them droop slightly backwards...

Now make a fist with your right hand.
Feel the tightness travel up from your wrist...
through the forearm, and upper arm, to your neck muscles...
And relax.
Now make a fist with your left hand,
again feeling the tightness in your forearm,
upper arm, neck muscles...
Again relaxing neck, shoulders, arm, wrist and hand.

With eyes still closed, slowly move your head and neck slightly,
from side to side... up and down...

until you find the most comfortable position.

Now become aware once more of your breathing,
your own ordinary breathing rhythm...
Don't force it or try to change it, just become aware of it.
Cool air breathed in, warm air breathed out... gently...
felt on your upper lip...

Now let the warm breath move aside the warm darkness, as in your
imagination, with eyes still closed, you allow yourself to enter the
meditation.

I am here...
You expected me...
I am your treasure...

I am here...
I knocked...
I am still doing so...

I am here...
You opened the door...
so now we can search...
together...

I name again my special wish
and hope

I bring my gaze to the centre of my being.
taking one phrase or word
from what Jesus has just said.
I let it be the promise on my breath...

🌺   *Ask, and it will be given you;*
       search, and you will find;
       knock, and the door will be opened for you.
       For everyone who asks receives,
🌺   *and everyone who searches finds,*
       and for everyone who knocks,
       the door will be opened…

🌺   His gift…
       My surprise…

🌺   Stay with this…

And now,
slowly begin to withdraw from the scene…
Begin to be aware of your body again,
slowly moving fingers…
toes…
Gently roll your head from side to side.
Take a deep breath,
and when you are ready,
slowly open your eyes, but just looking with soft eyes…

until you are ready to move out from this space,
for now.

15

Who Cares?

o he [Jesus] told them this parable: 'Which one of you, having a hundred sheep and losing one of them, does not leave the ninety-nine in the wilderness and go after the one that is lost until he finds it? When he has found it, he lays it on his shoulders and rejoices. And when he comes home, he calls together his friends and neighbours, saying to them, 'Rejoice with me, for I have found my sheep that was lost.' (Luke 15:3-6)

We now move from this passage into personal meditation,
starting off with some deep relaxation.
Whether you are sitting or lying down,
check that your body is comfortably positioned
and that you have enough space around you
to feel comfortable.
Acknowledge the fact of any sounds from inside or outside,
and then let them go…
Now, starting off by becoming aware of the points of contact
between your body and the chair or your body and the floor…
become aware of the chair or floor beneath you,
and allow it to support your body.
Relax any tightness of your tummy muscles on a slow out-breath…

warm air breathed out,
Then an in-breath, cool air breathed in,
felt on your upper lip...
Now, imagine yourself floating into warm darkness for a moment,
and allow your eyes to close.
Bring your attention down to your right foot...
Without moving the whole leg, just gently move your right ankle up and
down once or twice... then rest it again.
Still with the right foot, begin to tighten the muscles of your right calf...
and the muscles around your knee...
Hold the tension a moment or two, and then release it,
feeling that right leg relaxing and sinking.

Now, bringing your awareness to your left foot,
again gently move your ankle up and down once or twice, and then rest it.
Now just tighten the muscles of your left calf...
and the muscles around your left knee...
Hold the tension a moment or two, and then release it.
Feel the heaviness and relaxation in both legs and feet,
and check if they need to shift position at all.
If so, do so gently, and relax.

Now, on an out-breath, relax the tummy muscles around your waist...
Then let your shoulders relax by slightly lifting and then letting them
drop, or, if lying down, let them droop slightly backwards...

Now make a fist with your right hand.
Feel the tightness travel up from your wrist...
through the forearm, and upper arm, to your neck muscles...
And relax.
Now make a fist with your left hand,
again feeling the tightness in your forearm,
upper arm, neck muscles...
Again relaxing neck, shoulders, arm, wrist and hand.

With eyes still closed, slowly move your head and neck slightly,
from side to side… up and down…
until you find the most comfortable position.

Now become aware once more of your breathing,
your own ordinary breathing rhythm…
Don't force it or try to change it, just become aware of it.
Cool air breathed in, warm air breathed out… gently…
felt on your upper lip…

Now let the warm breath move aside the warm darkness, as in your
imagination, with eyes still closed, you allow yourself to enter the
meditation.

       The sheep is in a different place
       from where it usually is.
       What happened
       that it moved away?
       Where is it now?
       In my imagination I picture the place.

       Is it high up…
       or low down?
       Is it rocky?
       slippery?
       tangled?

       And if I was that sheep,
       would I recognise this place?
       Caught.
       Wanting rescue,
       yet actually not wanting it.
       Lost, but not so lost.
       Worried sometimes,

then not caring.
Who cares?

Then the words of the shepherd.
'I am the good shepherd.
I know my own, and my own know me.
I give them eternal life
and they will never perish.'

Eternal life?
Is this about longer-term happiness?

Am I happy?
Where?
Am I unhappy?
Where?

Your presence...
My inner freedom.

The invitation is there.
What am I resisting?
What can I hold on to?

This may not be losing something...
Perhaps I will find something
as the shepherd has found me.

I look at Jesus
as I imagine him to look,
dressed as I imagine him to be dressed,
and I listen to his voice.
Quietly...
Because perhaps
right now

I just don't know.
I can't come back on my own.
I wait for help
to lift me...

I allow myself to feel carried,
– and meanwhile
I can tell the shepherd
about coming home,
or perhaps it is enough just to be silent,
safely.

Stay with this...

And now,
slowly begin to withdraw from the scene...
Begin to be aware of your body again,
slowly moving fingers...
toes...
Gently roll your head from side to side.
Take a deep breath,
and when you are ready,
slowly open your eyes, but just looking with soft eyes...

until you are ready to move out from this space,
for now.

16

Worth It

esus took with him Peter and James and John, and led them up a high mountain apart, by themselves. And he was transfigured before them, and his clothes became dazzling white, such as no one on earth could bleach them. And there appeared to them Elijah with Moses, who were talking with Jesus. Then Peter said to Jesus, 'Rabbi, it is good for us to be here; let us make three dwellings, one for you, one for Moses, and one for Elijah.' He did not know what to say, for they were terrified. Then a cloud overshadowed them, and from the cloud there came a voice, 'This is my Son, the beloved; listen to him.' (Mark 9:2-7)

We now move from this passage into personal meditation,
starting off with some deep relaxation.
Whether you are sitting or lying down,
check that your body is comfortably positioned
and that you have enough space around you
to feel comfortable.
Acknowledge the fact of any sounds from inside or outside,
and then let them go...
Now, starting off by becoming aware of the points of contact

between your body and the chair or your body and the floor...
become aware of the chair or floor beneath you,
and allow it to support your body.
Relax any tightness of your tummy muscles on a slow out-breath...
warm air breathed out,
Then an in-breath, cool air breathed in,
felt on your upper lip...
Now, imagine yourself floating into warm darkness for a moment,
and allow your eyes to close.
Bring your attention down to your right foot...
Without moving the whole leg, just gently move your right ankle up and
down once or twice... then rest it again.
Still with the right foot, begin to tighten the muscles of your right calf...
and the muscles around your knee...
Hold the tension a moment or two, and then release it,
feeling that right leg relaxing and sinking.

Now, bringing your awareness to your left foot,
again gently move your ankle up and down once or twice, and then rest it.
Now just tighten the muscles of your left calf...
and the muscles around your left knee...
Hold the tension a moment or two, and then release it.
Feel the heaviness and relaxation in both legs and feet,
and check if they need to shift position at all.
If so, do so gently, and relax.

Now, on an out-breath, relax the tummy muscles around your waist...
Then let your shoulders relax by slightly lifting and then letting them
drop, or, if lying down, let them droop slightly backwards...

Now make a fist with your right hand.
Feel the tightness travel up from your wrist...
through the forearm, and upper arm, to your neck muscles...
And relax.
Now make a fist with your left hand,

again feeling the tightness in your forearm,
upper arm, neck muscles...
Again relaxing neck, shoulders, arm, wrist and hand.

With eyes still closed, slowly move your head and neck slightly,
from side to side... up and down...
until you find the most comfortable position.

Now become aware once more of your breathing,
your own ordinary breathing rhythm...
Don't force it or try to change it, just become aware of it.
Cool air breathed in, warm air breathed out... gently...
felt on your upper lip...

Now let the warm breath move aside the warm darkness, as in your
imagination, with eyes still closed, you allow yourself to enter the
meditation.

    You feel special.
        Whatever time of day it is,
        morning or afternoon,
        you are chosen to accompany Jesus
        up to this hilltop that you see ahead.

        Become aware of who your companions are...
        and the landscape you are leaving,
        and the one ahead...

        As you climb,
        notice how you feel about Jesus
        and how it feels to have him think of you as a
        friend...

And now you have arrived.
The space is yours.

Jesus gives you his full attention.
He has been talking about getting through hard
times.
He is facing into pain and betrayal.
Why is he telling you?
Perhaps he knows that you too, like Peter, James and
John,
have had your share of hard times...
as both of you recall.
You talk to him of these.

But Jesus is also seeing beyond the pain.
It isn't the end.
He asks you about your hopes for the future,
your dreams.

He listens,
and you have a sense that
he wants the best for you too.
That you and your dreams
are worth cosmic change.
Life and death...
and resurrection...

Seeing him this way,
bright with light,
so alive and yet able to connect with the past,
you sense that you too have a connection
with a wide tradition,
bigger and stronger than anything...

🌹 And it is clear he can be there with you...
to hold you through
any rough times ahead...
and he shows it
🌹 by surrounding you with light.

Just let that transfiguring light be around you,
Glowing...
🌹 Breathe it in...

Stay with this...

And now,
slowly begin to withdraw from the scene...
Begin to be aware of your body again,
slowly moving fingers...
toes...
Gently roll your head from side to side.
Take a deep breath,
and when you are ready,
slowly open your eyes, but just looking with soft eyes...

until you are ready to move out from this space,
for now.

17

Standing Straight

Now he [Jesus] was teaching in one of the synagogues on the sabbath. And just then there appeared a woman with a spirit that had crippled her for eighteen years. She was bent over and quite unable to stand up straight. When Jesus saw her, he called her over and said, 'Woman, you are set free from your ailment.' When he laid his hands on her, immediately she stood up straight and began praising God. (Luke 13:10-12)

We now move from this passage into personal meditation,
starting off with some deep relaxation.
Whether you are sitting or lying down,
check that your body is comfortably positioned
and that you have enough space around you
to feel comfortable.
Acknowledge the fact of any sounds from inside or outside,
and then let them go...
Now, starting off by becoming aware of the points of contact
between your body and the chair or your body and the floor...
become aware of the chair or floor beneath you,
and allow it to support your body.
Relax any tightness of your tummy muscles on a slow out-breath...

warm air breathed out,
Then an in-breath, cool air breathed in,
felt on your upper lip...
Now, imagine yourself floating into warm darkness for a moment,
and allow your eyes to close.
Bring your attention down to your right foot...
Without moving the whole leg, just gently move your right ankle up and
down once or twice... then rest it again.
Still with the right foot, begin to tighten the muscles of your right calf...
and the muscles around your knee...
Hold the tension a moment or two, and then release it,
feeling that right leg relaxing and sinking.

Now, bringing your awareness to your left foot,
again gently move your ankle up and down once or twice, and then rest it.
Now just tighten the muscles of your left calf...
and the muscles around your left knee...
Hold the tension a moment or two, and then release it.
Feel the heaviness and relaxation in both legs and feet,
and check if they need to shift position at all.
If so, do so gently, and relax.

Now, on an out-breath, relax the tummy muscles around your waist...
Then let your shoulders relax by slightly lifting and then letting them
drop, or, if lying down, let them droop slightly backwards...

Now make a fist with your right hand.
Feel the tightness travel up from your wrist...
through the forearm, and upper arm, to your neck muscles...
And relax.
Now make a fist with your left hand,
again feeling the tightness in your forearm,
upper arm, neck muscles...
Again relaxing neck, shoulders, arm, wrist and hand.

With eyes still closed, slowly move your head and neck slightly,
from side to side... up and down...
until you find the most comfortable position.

Now become aware once more of your breathing,
your own ordinary breathing rhythm...
Don't force it or try to change it, just become aware of it.
Cool air breathed in, warm air breathed out... gently...
felt on your upper lip...

Now let the warm breath move aside the warm darkness, as in your
imagination, with eyes still closed, you allow yourself to enter the
meditation.

You can see her, not too far away...
In your imagination, she takes the shape that has kept
her crippled in some way...
You are not afraid of her.

She seems gentle, so perhaps it is possible to
approach.

She is looking at Jesus, but then it seems she is also
looking at you.
'Are you here to be healed too?'
she seems to be asking.

Me?
I'm not crippled.

Is that too quick?

You begin to reflect.
Am I crippled in some way?
Handicapped in an invisible way
that makes it hard for me to stand straight?

Where in my life am I not straight?
With family?
A friend?
Myself?
Jesus?

But I'm used to the way I am.

'So was I',
the woman seems to say.

Is this a challenge?
Stay and talk to the Lord about this...

And now,
slowly begin to withdraw from the scene...
Begin to be aware of your body again,
slowly moving fingers...
toes...
Gently roll your head from side to side.
Take a deep breath,
and when you are ready,
slowly open your eyes, but just looking with soft eyes...

until you are ready to move out from this space,
for now.

18

Charity Appeals

hen [Jesus] came to Nazareth, where he had been brought up, he went to the synagogue on the sabbath day, as was his custom. He stood up to read, and the scroll of the prophet Isaiah was given to him. He unrolled the scroll and found the place where it was written: 'The Spirit of the Lord is upon me, because he has anointed me to bring good news to the poor. He has sent me to proclaim release to the captives and recovery of sight to the blind, to let the oppressed go free, to proclaim the year of the Lord's favour.' And he rolled up the scroll, gave it back to the attendant, and sat down. The eyes of all in the synagogue were fixed on him. Then he began to say to them, 'Today, this scripture has been fulfilled in your hearing.' (Luke 4:16-21)

We now move from this passage into personal meditation,
starting off with some deep relaxation.
Whether you are sitting or lying down,
check that your body is comfortably positioned
and that you have enough space around you
to feel comfortable.
Acknowledge the fact of any sounds from inside or outside,
and then let them go...

Now, starting off by becoming aware of the points of contact
between your body and the chair or your body and the floor...
become aware of the chair or floor beneath you,
and allow it to support your body.
Relax any tightness of your tummy muscles on a slow out-breath...
warm air breathed out,
Then an in-breath, cool air breathed in,
felt on your upper lip...
Now, imagine yourself floating into warm darkness for a moment,
and allow your eyes to close.
Bring your attention down to your right foot...
Without moving the whole leg, just gently move your right ankle up and
down once or twice... then rest it again.
Still with the right foot, begin to tighten the muscles of your right calf...
and the muscles around your knee...
Hold the tension a moment or two, and then release it,
feeling that right leg relaxing and sinking.

Now, bringing your awareness to your left foot,
again gently move your ankle up and down once or twice, and then rest it.
Now just tighten the muscles of your left calf...
and the muscles around your left knee...
Hold the tension a moment or two, and then release it.
Feel the heaviness and relaxation in both legs and feet,
and check if they need to shift position at all.
If so, do so gently, and relax.

Now, on an out-breath, relax the tummy muscles around your waist...
Then let your shoulders relax by slightly lifting and then letting them
drop, or, if lying down, let them droop slightly backwards...

Now make a fist with your right hand.
Feel the tightness travel up from your wrist...
through the forearm, and upper arm, to your neck muscles...
And relax.

Now make a fist with your left hand,
again feeling the tightness in your forearm,
upper arm, neck muscles...
Again relaxing neck, shoulders, arm, wrist and hand.

With eyes still closed, slowly move your head and neck slightly,
from side to side... up and down...
until you find the most comfortable position.

Now become aware once more of your breathing,
your own ordinary breathing rhythm...
Don't force it or try to change it, just become aware of it.
Cool air breathed in, warm air breathed out... gently...
felt on your upper lip...

Now let the warm breath move aside the warm darkness, as in your
imagination, with eyes still closed, you allow yourself to enter the
meditation.

It is crowded in the synagogue.
Become aware of the people,
men below, women in the gallery...
The large lectern
or Reader's stand.
Jesus, dressed as you imagine him to be dressed,
looking as you imagine him to look,
moving up to take the scroll of Scripture.
You see the sunlight through the door,
and the glow of it in the large room
You hear his words...
'Good news to the poor...'

You have heard so much about the poor
You think of the last television documentary that
featured poor children.

🌿 You wonder what is meant by the words:
'Jesus has come to bring good news to the poor.'
You imagine what it must be like to be that child on
the TV

🌿 or on the appeals poster...
Is Jesus with her? or him?
Or is he expecting you to be?

🌿 How?
When?
Or is there someone else to whom you are
being called to be good news?

🌿 Who comes to mind?
Your granny?
Your grandad,
that other girl

🌿 boy...
(man, woman, colleague)?

🌿 You ask... What do you mean, Lord?
I want to hear you.
Tell me how I can be good news...

Stay with this...

And now,
slowly begin to withdraw from the scene...
Begin to be aware of your body again,
slowly moving fingers...
toes...
Gently roll your head from side to side.
Take a deep breath,
and when you are ready,
slowly open your eyes, but just looking with soft eyes...

until you are ready to move out from this space,
for now.

19

Welcome to Where I Live

h e [Jesus] entered Jericho and was passing through it. A man was there named Zacchaeus; he was a chief tax-collector and was rich. He was trying to see who Jesus was, but on account of the crowd he could not, because he was short in stature. So he ran ahead and climbed a sycamore tree to see him, because he was going to pass that way. When Jesus came to the place, he looked up and said to him, 'Zacchaeus, hurry and come down; for I must stay at your house today.' So he hurried down and was happy to welcome him. (Luke 19:1-6)

We now move from this passage into personal meditation,
starting off with some deep relaxation.
Whether you are sitting or lying down,
check that your body is comfortably positioned
and that you have enough space around you
to feel comfortable.
Acknowledge the fact of any sounds from inside or outside,
and then let them go...
Now, starting off by becoming aware of the points of contact
between your body and the chair or your body and the floor...
become aware of the chair or floor beneath you,

and allow it to support your body.
Relax any tightness of your tummy muscles on a slow out-breath…
warm air breathed out,
Then an in-breath, cool air breathed in,
felt on your upper lip…
Now, imagine yourself floating into warm darkness for a moment,
and allow your eyes to close.
Bring your attention down to your right foot…
Without moving the whole leg, just gently move your right ankle up and
down once or twice… then rest it again.
Still with the right foot, begin to tighten the muscles of your right calf…
and the muscles around your knee…
Hold the tension a moment or two, and then release it,
feeling that right leg relaxing and sinking.

Now, bringing your awareness to your left foot,
again gently move your ankle up and down once or twice, and then rest it.
Now just tighten the muscles of your left calf…
and the muscles around your left knee…
Hold the tension a moment or two, and then release it.
Feel the heaviness and relaxation in both legs and feet,
and check if they need to shift position at all.
If so, do so gently, and relax.

Now, on an out-breath, relax the tummy muscles around your waist…
Then let your shoulders relax by slightly lifting and then letting them
drop, or, if lying down, let them droop slightly backwards…

Now make a fist with your right hand.
Feel the tightness travel up from your wrist…
through the forearm, and upper arm, to your neck muscles…
And relax.
Now make a fist with your left hand,
again feeling the tightness in your forearm,
upper arm, neck muscles…
Again relaxing neck, shoulders, arm, wrist and hand.

With eyes still closed, slowly move your head and neck slightly,
from side to side... up and down...
until you find the most comfortable position.

Now become aware once more of your breathing,
your own ordinary breathing rhythm...
Don't force it or try to change it, just become aware of it.
Cool air breathed in, warm air breathed out... gently...
felt on your upper lip...

Now let the warm breath move aside the warm darkness, as in your
imagination, with eyes still closed, you allow yourself to enter the
meditation.

I have come to this place...
and I have not yet seen Jesus...
It made sense to climb up into the tree with
Zacchaeus.

He is too small to see...
The crowd laughed...
He didn't care.
Kept climbing...
They might laugh at me too,
for some reason...
Do I care?

Up here, with the leaves all around like protection,
what do I expect to see?
If I do see Jesus, do I want to speak to him?
Would he want to speak to me?

But he is already here, calling up to Zacchaeus,
inviting himself to a meal.

❀   I would like to invite him myself.
         He is still below.

         If it feels real, I can do so.
❀   'Come and see where I live.
         Now.'

         It is easy to find the way...
❀   we go inside...
         he is respectful...
         it is up to me to show him...
❀   He asks if there is anything I especially want to say
         to him.

         He listens...
❀   I talk.
         He forgives...
         We laugh.

❀   Stay with this...

And now,
slowly begin to withdraw from the scene...
Begin to be aware of your body again,
slowly moving fingers...
toes...
Gently roll your head from side to side.
Take a deep breath,
and when you are ready,
slowly open your eyes, but just looking with soft eyes...

until you are ready to move out from this space,
for now.

20

Walking With Loss

Now on that same day two of [the disciples] were going to a
village called Emmaus, about seven miles from Jerusalem,
and talking with each other about all these things that had
happened. While they were talking and discussing, Jesus
himself came near and went with them, but their eyes were kept
from recognizing him. And he said to them, 'What are you
discussing with each other as you walk along?' They stood still...
Then one of them... answered him... [Then] he interpreted to them
the things about himself in all the scriptures. (Luke 24:13-18, 27)

We now move from this passage into personal meditation,
starting off with some deep relaxation.
Whether you are sitting or lying down,
check that your body is comfortably positioned
and that you have enough space around you
to feel comfortable.
Acknowledge the fact of any sounds from inside or outside,
and then let them go...
Now, starting off by becoming aware of the points of contact
between your body and the chair or your body and the floor...
become aware of the chair or floor beneath you,

and allow it to support your body.
Relax any tightness of your tummy muscles on a slow out-breath…
warm air breathed out,
Then an in-breath, cool air breathed in,
felt on your upper lip…
Now, imagine yourself floating into warm darkness for a moment,
and allow your eyes to close.
Bring your attention down to your right foot…
Without moving the whole leg, just gently move your right ankle up and
down once or twice… then rest it again.
Still with the right foot, begin to tighten the muscles of your right calf…
and the muscles around your knee…
Hold the tension a moment or two, and then release it,
feeling that right leg relaxing and sinking.

Now, bringing your awareness to your left foot,
again gently move your ankle up and down once or twice, and then rest it.
Now just tighten the muscles of your left calf…
and the muscles around your left knee…
Hold the tension a moment or two, and then release it.
Feel the heaviness and relaxation in both legs and feet,
and check if they need to shift position at all.
If so, do so gently, and relax.

Now, on an out-breath, relax the tummy muscles around your waist…
Then let your shoulders relax by slightly lifting and then letting them
drop, or, if lying down, let them droop slightly backwards…

Now make a fist with your right hand.
Feel the tightness travel up from your wrist…
through the forearm, and upper arm, to your neck muscles…
And relax.
Now make a fist with your left hand,
again feeling the tightness in your forearm,
upper arm, neck muscles…

Again relaxing neck, shoulders, arm, wrist and hand.

With eyes still closed, slowly move your head and neck slightly,
from side to side... up and down...
until you find the most comfortable position.

Now become aware once more of your breathing,
your own ordinary breathing rhythm...
Don't force it or try to change it, just become aware of it.
Cool air breathed in, warm air breathed out... gently...
felt on your upper lip...

Now let the warm breath move aside the warm darkness, as in your
imagination, with eyes still closed, you allow yourself to enter the
meditation.

Loss.
They are experiencing the feelings that go with loss.
You may feel you can join them...
You hear what it is like...
although you may already know.
The loneliness,
the numbness,
the confusion,
moments of anger...

Jesus falls into step beside you.
He lets you tell him once again
the circumstances...
How it happened...
When... and where...
How it was and is for you now...

Allow him to be there.

Feel…
                        Wait…
                        Listen…

    Stay with this…

And now,
slowly begin to withdraw from the scene…
Begin to be aware of your body again,
slowly moving fingers…
toes…
Gently roll your head from side to side.
Take a deep breath,
and when you are ready,
slowly open your eyes, but just looking with soft eyes…

until you are ready to move out from this space,
for now.

21

Jesus, Me and Mass

s they came near the village to which they were going, he walked ahead as if he were going on. But they urged him strongly, saying, 'Stay with us, because it is almost evening and the day is now nearly over.' So he went in to stay with them. When he was at the table with them, he took bread, blessed and broke it, and gave it to them. Then their eyes were opened, and they recognised him...' (Luke 24:28-31)

We now move from this passage into personal meditation,
starting off with some deep relaxation.
Whether you are sitting or lying down,
check that your body is comfortably positioned
and that you have enough space around you
to feel comfortable.
Acknowledge the fact of any sounds from inside or outside,
and then let them go...
Now, starting off by becoming aware of the points of contact
between your body and the chair or your body and the floor...
become aware of the chair or floor beneath you,
and allow it to support your body.
Relax any tightness of your tummy muscles on a slow out-breath...

warm air breathed out,
Then an in-breath, cool air breathed in,
felt on your upper lip...
Now, imagine yourself floating into warm darkness for a moment,
and allow your eyes to close.
Bring your attention down to your right foot...
Without moving the whole leg, just gently move your right ankle up and
down once or twice... then rest it again.
Still with the right foot, begin to tighten the muscles of your right calf...
and the muscles around your knee...
Hold the tension a moment or two, and then release it,
feeling that right leg relaxing and sinking.

Now, bringing your awareness to your left foot,
again gently move your ankle up and down once or twice, and then rest it.
Now just tighten the muscles of your left calf...
and the muscles around your left knee...
Hold the tension a moment or two, and then release it.
Feel the heaviness and relaxation in both legs and feet,
and check if they need to shift position at all.
If so, do so gently, and relax.

Now, on an out-breath, relax the tummy muscles around your waist...
Then let your shoulders relax by slightly lifting and then letting them
drop, or, if lying down, let them droop slightly backwards...

Now make a fist with your right hand.
Feel the tightness travel up from your wrist...
through the forearm, and upper arm, to your neck muscles...
And relax.
Now make a fist with your left hand,
again feeling the tightness in your forearm,
upper arm, neck muscles...
Again relaxing neck, shoulders, arm, wrist and hand.

With eyes still closed, slowly move your head and neck slightly,
from side to side... up and down...
until you find the most comfortable position.

Now become aware once more of your breathing,
your own ordinary breathing rhythm...
Don't force it or try to change it, just become aware of it.
Cool air breathed in, warm air breathed out... gently...
felt on your upper lip...

Now let the warm breath move aside the warm darkness, as in your
imagination, with eyes still closed, you allow yourself to enter the
meditation.

I find myself moving
with the two disciples through the door,
but it isn't what I expected...
It seems to be the place where I might go to Mass...
In imagination, I see this place
large, or small,
dark or light...
Any special features?

Past and present merge,
and I am meeting Jesus in the Eucharist.
First I find myself looking into my heart:
how do I come?
what are my feelings?
what am I expecting?

I listen to the Word of Scripture,
the passage that tells me he is with me at all times,
even to the end of the world.

I see him taking up bread,
offering it...
taking the cup of wine, offering it...
I hear him praying for me,
I hear him praying for my family,
my friends...
I hear him remembering those who have died.

I hear him
pray the Our Father.
Slowly, phrase by phrase.

Our Father...
who art in heaven...

hallowed be thy name...

Thy kingdom come...

thy will be done on earth...
as it is in heaven...

Give us this day...
our daily bread...

and forgive us our trespasses...
as we forgive those...
who trespass against us...

and lead us not into temptation...
but deliver us from evil...

for thine is the kingdom,
the power and the glory
for ever and ever, Amen.

I think about forever…
and then I hear the offer and promise of peace.
I stretch out my hand,
and with it, my heart,
and so I am receiving Jesus.

In this moment,
like the disciples,
I recognise him.

Stay with this…

And now,
slowly begin to withdraw from the scene…
Begin to be aware of your body again,
slowly moving fingers…
toes…
Gently roll your head from side to side.
Take a deep breath,
and when you are ready,
slowly open your eyes, but just looking with soft eyes…

until you are ready to move out from this space,
for now.

22

Presence

hile they were talking about [Jesus rising from the dead], Jesus himself stood among them and said to them, 'Peace be with you.' They were startled and terrified, and thought they were seeing a ghost. He said to them, 'Why are you frightened, and why do doubts arise in your hearts? Look at my hands and my feet; see that it is I myself. (Luke 24:36-41)

We now move from this passage into personal meditation,
starting off with some deep relaxation.
Whether you are sitting or lying down,
check that your body is comfortably positioned
and that you have enough space around you
to feel comfortable.
Acknowledge the fact of any sounds from inside or outside,
and then let them go...
Now, starting off by becoming aware of the points of contact
between your body and the chair or your body and the floor...
become aware of the chair or floor beneath you,
and allow it to support your body.
Relax any tightness of your tummy muscles on a slow out-breath...
warm air breathed out,

Then an in-breath, cool air breathed in,
felt on your upper lip...
Now, imagine yourself floating into warm darkness for a moment,
and allow your eyes to close.
Bring your attention down to your right foot...
Without moving the whole leg, just gently move your right ankle up and
down once or twice... then rest it again.
Still with the right foot, begin to tighten the muscles of your right calf...
and the muscles around your knee...
Hold the tension a moment or two, and then release it,
feeling that right leg relaxing and sinking.

Now, bringing your awareness to your left foot,
again gently move your ankle up and down once or twice, and then rest it.
Now just tighten the muscles of your left calf...
and the muscles around your left knee...
Hold the tension a moment or two, and then release it.
Feel the heaviness and relaxation in both legs and feet,
and check if they need to shift position at all.
If so, do so gently, and relax.

Now, on an out-breath, relax the tummy muscles around your waist...
Then let your shoulders relax by slightly lifting and then letting them
drop, or, if lying down, let them droop slightly backwards...

Now make a fist with your right hand.
Feel the tightness travel up from your wrist...
through the forearm, and upper arm, to your neck muscles...
And relax.
Now make a fist with your left hand,
again feeling the tightness in your forearm,
upper arm, neck muscles...
Again relaxing neck, shoulders, arm, wrist and hand.

With eyes still closed, slowly move your head and neck slightly,

from side to side... up and down...
until you find the most comfortable position.

Now become aware once more of your breathing,
your own ordinary breathing rhythm...
Don't force it or try to change it, just become aware of it.
Cool air breathed in, warm air breathed out... gently...
felt on your upper lip...

Now let the warm breath move aside the warm darkness, as in your
imagination, with eyes still closed, you allow yourself to enter the
meditation.

It seems impossible,
but what you can see,
here in this room,
is Jesus after the Resurrection...
Notice how he looks...
and what he says to Thomas,
and to you...

That he is here in the room is hard to believe,
but is it any harder
than believing he is in the circumstances
of ordinary life?

Jesus in the ordinary circumstances of your life.
How could that be possible?
That's much too small...
There's no point praying about that.
Perhaps he thinks there is...
You can ask him...

You look at Jesus,
That's what you hoped he would be like,
and he is...
but, like Thomas, you find it hard to trust this.

Yet Jesus reminds you of the times
when he was there
and you didn't realise it until afterwards...
You remember...

He then reminds you of the times
he was there, and yes,
You were somehow aware of it...
You remember...

You can go back over these moments together
for as long as you need,

Stay with this...

And now,
slowly begin to withdraw from the scene...
Begin to be aware of your body again,
slowly moving fingers...
toes...
Gently roll your head from side to side.
Take a deep breath,
and when you are ready,
slowly open your eyes, but just looking with soft eyes...

until you are ready to move out from this space,
for now.

23

A New Day

esus showed himself again to the disciples by the Sea of Tiberias;... Just after daybreak, Jesus stood on the beach; but the disciples did not know that it was Jesus. Jesus said to them, 'Children, you have no fish, have you? They answered him, 'No.' He said to them, 'Cast the net to the right side of the boat, and you will find some.' So they cast it, and now they were not able to haul it in because there were so many fish. That disciple whom Jesus loved said to Peter, 'It is the Lord!' When Simon Peter heard [this], he jumped into the sea. But the other disciples came in the boat, dragging the net full of fish, for they were not far from the land...

When they had gone ashore, they saw a charcoal fire there, with fish on it, and bread. Jesus said to them, 'Bring some of the fish that you have just caught. So Simon Peter went aboard and hauled the net ashore, full of large fish.... Jesus said to them, 'Come and have breakfast.' (John 21:1, 4-12)

We now move from this passage into personal meditation,
starting off with some deep relaxation.
Whether you are sitting or lying down,
check that your body is comfortably positioned

and that you have enough space around you
to feel comfortable.
Acknowledge the fact of any sounds from inside or outside,
and then let them go...
Now, starting off by becoming aware of the points of contact
between your body and the chair or your body and the floor...
become aware of the chair or floor beneath you,
and allow it to support your body.
Relax any tightness of your tummy muscles on a slow out-breath...
warm air breathed out,
Then an in-breath, cool air breathed in,
felt on your upper lip...
Now, imagine yourself floating into warm darkness for a moment,
and allow your eyes to close.
Bring your attention down to your right foot...
Without moving the whole leg, just gently move your right ankle up and
down once or twice... then rest it again.
Still with the right foot, begin to tighten the muscles of your right calf...
and the muscles around your knee...
Hold the tension a moment or two, and then release it,
feeling that right leg relaxing and sinking.

Now, bringing your awareness to your left foot,
again gently move your ankle up and down once or twice, and then rest it.
Now just tighten the muscles of your left calf...
and the muscles around your left knee...
Hold the tension a moment or two, and then release it.
Feel the heaviness and relaxation in both legs and feet,
and check if they need to shift position at all.
If so, do so gently, and relax.

Now, on an out-breath, relax the tummy muscles around your waist...
Then let your shoulders relax by slightly lifting and then letting them
drop, or, if lying down, let them droop slightly backwards...

Now make a fist with your right hand.
Feel the tightness travel up from your wrist...
through the forearm, and upper arm, to your neck muscles...
And relax.
Now make a fist with your left hand,
again feeling the tightness in your forearm,
upper arm, neck muscles...
Again relaxing neck, shoulders, arm, wrist and hand.

With eyes still closed, slowly move your head and neck slightly,
from side to side... up and down...
until you find the most comfortable position.

Now become aware once more of your breathing,
your own ordinary breathing rhythm...
Don't force it or try to change it, just become aware of it.
Cool air breathed in, warm air breathed out... gently...
felt on your upper lip...

Now let the warm breath move aside the warm darkness, as in your
imagination, with eyes still closed, you allow yourself to enter the
meditation.

It is just approaching dawn.
An apricot sky, with grey flecks, and I am afloat in my
own little world.
Up and down on the slow swell of the sea...
same view, same people...
Is this all I want?
Content to be here...

Is anything missing?
I reflect on the present space I am in.

How does it feel?

I look across the prow of the boat...
a figure, there on the shore...

Who tells me it is Jesus?

It is the Lord!
Where have I felt or known this before in my life?

He is calling my name...
Do I want to respond?

Is he asking me to take a risk?
To break out of that part of me that stays safely on
board?

Do I dare to jump into the water?
If I do, I find
It isn't too deep.

He is encouraging...
I reach the shore...

He invites me to break the long time of fasting.

Have I been fasting?
Keeping something away?
Do I want what he offers?

What might this mean?

Come and have breakfast, he says...
What are you offering me, Lord?

�)   I am there.
      I reach out my hand...
      I come to the fire...
      I receive the warmth and food from his hand...
🌒   and I hear the words that go with it.

      We talk...

🌒   Stay with this...

And now,
slowly begin to withdraw from the scene...
Begin to be aware of your body again,
slowly moving fingers...
toes...
Gently roll your head from side to side.
Take a deep breath,
and when you are ready,
slowly open your eyes, but just looking with soft eyes...

until you are ready to move out from this space,
for now.

24

What Do You Want Me To Do?

hen [Jesus and the disciples] had finished breakfast, Jesus said to Simon Peter, 'Simon son of John, do you love me more than these?' He said to him, 'Yes, Lord; you know that I love you.' Jesus said to him, 'Feed my lambs.' A second time he said to him, 'Simon son of John, do you love me?' He said to him, 'Yes, Lord; you know that I love you.' Jesus said to him, 'Tend my sheep.' He said to him the third time, 'Simon son of John, do you love me?' And he said to him, 'Lord, you know everything ... you know that I love you.' Jesus said to him, 'Feed my sheep.' (John 21:15-17)

We now move from this passage into personal meditation,
starting off with some deep relaxation.
Whether you are sitting or lying down,
check that your body is comfortably positioned
and that you have enough space around you
to feel comfortable.
Acknowledge the fact of any sounds from inside or outside,
and then let them go...
Now, starting off by becoming aware of the points of contact
between your body and the chair or your body and the floor...

become aware of the chair or floor beneath you,
and allow it to support your body.
Relax any tightness of your tummy muscles on a slow out-breath...
warm air breathed out,
Then an in-breath, cool air breathed in,
felt on your upper lip...
Now, imagine yourself floating into warm darkness for a moment,
and allow your eyes to close.
Bring your attention down to your right foot...
Without moving the whole leg, just gently move your right ankle up and
down once or twice... then rest it again.
Still with the right foot, begin to tighten the muscles of your right calf...
and the muscles around your knee...
Hold the tension a moment or two, and then release it,
feeling that right leg relaxing and sinking.

Now, bringing your awareness to your left foot,
again gently move your ankle up and down once or twice, and then rest it.
Now just tighten the muscles of your left calf...
and the muscles around your left knee...
Hold the tension a moment or two, and then release it.
Feel the heaviness and relaxation in both legs and feet,
and check if they need to shift position at all.
If so, do so gently, and relax.

Now, on an out-breath, relax the tummy muscles around your waist...
Then let your shoulders relax by slightly lifting and then letting them
drop, or, if lying down, let them droop slightly backwards...

Now make a fist with your right hand.
Feel the tightness travel up from your wrist...
through the forearm, and upper arm, to your neck muscles...
And relax.
Now make a fist with your left hand,
again feeling the tightness in your forearm,

upper arm, neck muscles...
Again relaxing neck, shoulders, arm, wrist and hand.

With eyes still closed, slowly move your head and neck slightly,
from side to side... up and down...
until you find the most comfortable position.

Now become aware once more of your breathing,
your own ordinary breathing rhythm...
Don't force it or try to change it, just become aware of it.
Cool air breathed in, warm air breathed out... gently...
felt on your upper lip...

Now let the warm breath move aside the warm darkness, as in your
imagination, with eyes still closed, you allow yourself to enter the
meditation.

Breakfast on the beach is over...
You smell the smoke from the fire.
A lovely, charcoal smell...
Let it surround you...
memories...

The disciples are relaxing now,
they have the boats in,
and soon they will sort the catch,
but they have eaten and now there is a pause.

Jesus looks across at you...
He invites you over...
How do you feel about this?
He looks at you...
tells you how much you matter.

He has already shown Peter this,
gave him time to talk... to sort out past mistakes,
and John, looking to his future,
and now it's your turn.

He tells you he knows you have a future...
asks you how you see it...
He knows what is important to you.
but he lets you tell him anyway.

He has asked Peter about love,
how he can show it to others.
Now you ask Jesus yourself
whom do I love?
who would know I love them?
how does it show?
what do I do?
or not do?

You reflect on those who love you...

You reflect on God's love for you...

You thank God for the gift of life

Stay with this...

And now,
slowly begin to withdraw from the scene...
Begin to be aware of your body again,
slowly moving fingers...
toes...
Gently roll your head from side to side.
Take a deep breath,